ROMANTICISM &
ESOTERIC TRADITION

ROMANTICISM & ESOTERIC TRADITION

Studies in Imagination

PAUL DAVIES

 Lindisfarne Books

This book is dedicated to the memory of

BULENT RAUF

(1911–1987)

Copyright © Paul Davies, 1998

Published by Lindisfarne Books
3390 Route 9, Hudson, NY 12534 USA

Library of Congress Cataloging-in-Publication Data
Davies, Paul, 1962–
Romanticism and esoteric tradition : studies in imagination / Paul Davies.
p. cm. — (Studies in imagination)
Includes bibliographical references and index.
ISBN 0-940262-88-6
1. Romanticism. 2. Spiritual life in literature. I. Title. II. Series.
PN751.D38 1998
820.9'145—dc21   97–47417
CIP

10 9 8 7 6 5 4 3 2 1

Printed in the United States of America

CONTENTS

Acknowledgments

The Faculty of Humanities at the University of Ulster generously provided a period of leave for writing and research. Many people have helped me, in all sorts of ways, during the time this book was being prepared. Besides debts to Terry, Antonia, and Mark Davies, I owe special thanks to Kathleen Raine, Richard MacEwan, Jane Plastow, Frances Rankin-Hutera, Aaron Cass, Arthur Martin, Julian Watson, Peter Young, Philip Wilson, Anna McMullan, Andrew and Karin Simpson-Parker, Gail and Gareth Baylis, Andrew Tomlinson, Hiroë Kaji, Paul Irwing, Jan Elliott, Patrick Welsh, Anne Wittman, Richard Bradford, John Newton, Anthony and Gillian Davis, John McVeagh, Barbara Skinner, Jeremy Mitchell; also thanks to Richard Geldard, and to Christopher Bamford and all those at Lindisfarne Books for helping to bring this book out. Needless to say, any errors and inadequacies are my responsibility.

Paul Davies

Preface

The introduction is an attempt to say why this book was written. The other nine essays are intended to allow, in some small degree, an instancing and reflection, as well as a study, of their subject. Therefore, beyond the introduction, I have spent less time arguing for the approach taken, and more time trying to gain maximum proximity to the themes themselves.

A number of links between chapters are indicated by cross-references, so that if the book is read in a different order from that printed, an appropriate, if not linear, continuity may be established.

The notes at the end of the book, almost without exception, are references and sources, intended solely to help the reader who may wish to pursue a reference or quotation further. The argument does not depend on the notes being consulted as they appear.

INTRODUCTION

Without the help of poets, what can the philosopher (…)
do if he persists in talking about the imagination?

—BACHELARD

In 1819 Shelley, feeling a combination of the deadly burden of the materialism overcoming his world, the tragic derelictions of his personal life, and the first inklings of ageing and death, finished the "Ode to the West Wind," one of the greatest poems ever written in English.

> Make me thy lyre, even as the forest is:
> What if my leaves are falling like its own!
> The tumult of thy mighty harmonies
>
> Will take from both a deep, autumnal tone,
> Sweet though in sadness. Be thou, spirit fierce
> My spirit! Be thou me, impetuous one!
>
> Drive my dead thoughts over the universe
> Like withered leaves to quicken a new birth!
> And, by the incantation of this verse,
>
> Scatter, as from an unextinguished hearth
> Ashes and sparks, my words among mankind!
> Be through my lips to unawakened earth
>
> The trumpet of a prophecy! O Wind,
> If Winter comes, can Spring be far behind?

Few utterances in poetry have ever been more sure of their balance on the borderline between the living and the dying, nor, by virtue of that very fact, been more instinct with the power of the new.

We are experiencing hunger for a new world as much during this age as the Romantics did in theirs, when the phrases "new age" and "new world" were on everyone's lips. This book is about the relationship between creativity—what Shelley called "the poetical faculty," "the poetry of life"[1]—and the teachings of the world's esoteric traditions. Its argument is that certain kinds of art, certain kinds of poetry, are the effective expression of a nonsectarian spiritual impulse that underlies the religious traditions of the world and holds potential for our evolution.

To show how this expression arises it is necessary to explore both the art and the esoteric teaching. I do not take the view of many present humanists that the arts are diversions, escapes, or amusements that help us avoid the "realities" of our existence. Nor that the arts should be seen as a territory of codes shared only by specialists, minimizing contact with a supposed "outside world." On the contrary, as Wordsworth said, poets do not write only for each other, but for humanity at large. The need of this time is to see how the impulse present in creative activity is noetic, teaching us about reality rather than suggesting an escape from it. But before it teaches us about reality, it must do the most difficult work of all—allow in us a *reorientation* in respect of reality. Art, far from sidestepping the real, is connected in all sorts of ways to the springs of knowledge and compassion, and once we taste even a trace of it we have no wish to escape it, but rather move to deepen our contact with it still further.

Why bring in the esoteric tradition? Isn't the pleasure of poetry, say, enough as it is, without speaking of a whole lot more? Art should not be turned into a kind of religion. This is an objection I often hear, and one with which I have every sympathy if, by "turned into religion," we mean allying with one camp against another, or substituting an outworn dogma with a novelty no less dogmatic. But it seems to me that our

---

conception of the pleasure of art has in this half century become so commodified and almost trivial that it doesn't fairly describe or resonate with our strongest actual responses to creative activity and to impulses that find expression in art. The effects of "the poetry of life" seem to me to be not so much celebrated as condescended to by the arts press and even by experts, scholars, and others whose voice is supposed to be in favor of creativity. Today, just as Shelley remarked of his own time, "It is admitted that the exercise of the imagination is most delightful, but it is alleged that that of reason is more useful."[2] So although I do not wish art to be understood to be a form of religion, I believe it is possible to go beyond religion and art when one touches the roots of creativity itself, and on the rarest of fortunate occasions experiences one's own being as the outflowing of that creative energy which is beyond religion but expressed through it, beyond art but making its presence felt in it. To touch the roots of religion and the roots of art is to feel not only the qualities proper to those expressions but also something basic and real about the one being that makes us and is us.

The possibility of contact with the roots of religion and art is one of the results of paying attention to the esoteric traditions, and is increasingly relevant to the world we live in now. The aim of the esoteric tradition is a right relationship with reality, which means studying it afresh, and questioning the subjective and pseudo-objective conditionings that we have used to define our lives, conditionings hidden in words like *real world* and *self* and *identity*. The esoteric teaching reverses many of these assumptions, and speaks to us with greater urgency of things which without its presence would still be dawning on us, but all too slowly, as (oddly) our exploitation of people and natural environment continues to accelerate.

One of the most fruitful ideas present both in esoteric teachings and in the thought of the Romantic period is the idea that it is especially, indeed almost only, in creativity that we

---

become able to receive into our present awareness impulses *from the future.* Whereas conventional historical thinking invites us to learn from our past mistakes, the attitude encouraged by esoteric education is receptivity to what is potential but not yet manifest, to what seeks to bring itself about through the agency of creativity. According to Edward Matchett, "in every true thought the known and the unknown come into contact[.] The principal regions of the unknown do not as yet have any material existence in any form whatever."[3] When Shelley wrote that poets are "hierophants of an unapprehended inspiration, the mirrors of the gigantic shadows which futurity casts upon the present,"[4] he was saying something in effect no different from Matchett, nor from the physicist David Bohm's suggestion of an implicate order in reality whose nature is to become explicate.[5] Anthony Blake puts it another way. "The future is the initiator of action," he says, "in which the future is made by the future itself. In ordinary language, this is creativity, but people do not understand the meaning of the word."[6]

The esoteric discipline and tradition is aimed specifically at ways of allowing this creative movement to happen. It is not only in consonance with ecology, but extends its perspective inward to clarify consciousness, as well as outward to the physical environment. This extension is inevitable, and more and more obviously so. For if existence is a whole, it must be present in the inner as well as the outer world, if indeed it allows us to speak of inner and outer in any terms but the most superficial. Any separation on a fundamental level of being would deny the axiom of wholeness. The precondition for sensitivity to what is continually requesting actualisation from the future is a complete recognition of the order of existence, which begins in the affirmation of the unity of all existence, knowing that existence is one and essentially indivisible. From that axiom all else ramifies, branches out, blossoms, comes into manifestation. Esoteric

———

teaching stresses that this perspective can take its extraordinary creative effect only in conditions where all doubt has ceased. The mystic's journey has stages during which elements of doubt and lack of knowledge are gradually purged and burnt away, and the surface of reflection continually polished. It is no coincidence that such a journey is also the Romantic poets' principal image of the meaningful course of life.

Philosophy, Psychology, and Esoterics in the Twentieth Century

Cultural ecosystems go wrong just as physical ones do when the ideas applied in them are not in the right relationship to reality. The fortunes of philosophy, for example, seem on the brink of extinction in the age we are coming to see as the post-modern. As culture goes through an ever-swifter transformation, some modern philosophers are announcing the death of philosophy.[7] Assuming the Cartesian and analytical traditions are meant, there can be no disputing that the time has come for something else. In reply to the question *What?* there opens an empty space. Viewed negatively, it is nihilism, the post-modern condition. Viewed positively, it is an opportunity. The intellectual foundations of the esoteric schools—foundations described in the treatises of metaphysicians and initiates, and equally, the experiential *modus vivendi* of poetic creation and spiritual practice—now have the opportunity to arise together in vigorous growth over the corpse of analytical philosophy. The upsurge of interest, everywhere in the West, in what is called the New Age counterculture might soon be recognized to have a sound basis in tradition, and to have something to offer to the culture which it counters, a culture in many ways foundering and, failing a radical renewal, devoid of further hope.

Over the last few decades, "depth" psychology has become involved with the study of culture and literary art. Perhaps this reflects a need to relate interpretation as such to the therapeutic function, not just to the intellectual. This trend is evidence in turn of a more far-reaching impulse, the wish to relate our interpretations of art, fiction, philosophical enquiry, and so on, to some of the central concerns of human life, to what are sometimes called "humanistic perspectives." Something similar might be said for the Marxist or Feminist whose intention is to stimulate people into political awareness or action. In psychology the concern is to counter psychological damage; in the case of socialism and feminism it is to be consciously and critically active in the social and economic world, in what is called the class or gender "struggle." But the intention of mystical philosophy and esoteric tradition is to go back another stage and re-learn what the nature of the human being is in its essence, before presuming what humanistic perspectives consist of. Humanism as it stands at the moment strives to protect the rights of the human conceived as an elaborate machine or at most a "social animal," but this is not enough.

It is becoming clearer and clearer throughout the world that the inner traditions of esoteric education address the issues pertinent to humanistic perspectives, but go much deeper and further than the others in their radical statements and studies of the premises on which all human activity and thought stand. (*Radical* is intended here in its original sense of penetration to the root, rather than in its popular sense of anti-establishment.) Although esoteric education is active on the historical plane, with abundant historical traces to be found,[8] it is not really delimited by history as the other humanistic perspectives, owing to their recent origin, seem to have been. The principles of the esoteric process have been enunciated, practiced and studied since written records began, and by all accounts from long before the time of literacy. The methods given, for example, in the East by Tibetan Buddhism, in central Asia and the Middle East by the Sufi schools, and in the West by the Rosicrucian, have been (to borrow the terms of

———

Leibniz, Aldous Huxley and many more after them) a truly *perennial* philosophy. Like the living stock of a plant, what William Blake called the "true vine of eternity,"[9] this tradition and method has been in constant use, sometimes emerging conspicuously into history, sometimes going underground, sometimes associated with the most prominent historical figures, sometimes so hidden as to attract the designation "occult." The same may come to apply to psychology of the Jungian and post-Jungian type, with its central uses of myths and dreams. Jung perhaps invented a contemporary formulation of a universal matter which he claimed little more than to have touched the edge of, rediscovered, brought to light. But that does not apply to the other "humanistic" processes. Only the *philosophia perennis* is trans-historical and ultimately trans-finite.

Since it is often experts on both sides of an argument who take contrary positions, there can be no more profit in elaborating defences of the practice of spiritual hermeneutics, which I employ in these essays on poetry, than there is use, for example, in the Freudians' justifying themselves to the Jungians while refuting the Reichians before feeling fit to undertake any consideration of psychology. The intention of this kind of study is not to win a debate, but to deepen the stages of awareness implicit in the study and practice of the arts, mysticism, and philosophy. My outline of the esoteric context throughout the following chapters and its resonance with the writings of some of the Romantic poets may serve as its own justification if justification is sought. It is difficult to plead any other in a culture whose latest epithet, *post-modern*, is almost synonymous with the inexorable vying of ideologies. To invest all one's efforts and enterprise into refutations and justifications is misplaced for another reason. However indomitably the writer may have researched and documented, the lists of evidence he can adduce will be respected only provided the vagaries of intellectual fashion have not outlawed the material cited as source. We are brought

———

inevitably to the conclusion that no text in itself will ever suffice as evidence or as source, and this not only because of a histori-cally-determined critical climate, but also because a text is usu-ally no more than comment about a matter, very seldom directly *from* it. And yet it is to the latter state, interestingly, that poetry and prophecy alike lay a claim. And where *gnosis* is the word for direct knowledge of states, *gnosiology* is probably the best term to use for a study of the ways of this direct knowledge. The chap-ters that follow are an attempt at such a study.

Historical records, the favorite of twentieth century academe, are not the only field of demonstration and interpretation. As Henry Corbin's works reveal so well, *homology of content* goes far beyond the connections verifiable by historical "causation." The recurrence of contents from traditions separated by large tracts of time and space offers real illumination to anyone contacting these contents with what Shelley called "a perception of resem-blances": namely, that the mutations and inherent mutability of forms, or "dress," which history can chart do not affect the per-manent living nature of the dressed, nor, for that matter, of the Addressed. "Truth is one, whatever clothes it wears."[10] The taste for similitude which many of the Romantics saw as the deepest significance of poetic creation is what furnishes true philosophi-cal knowledge, according to the perspective of Corbin and other practitioners of spiritual hermeneutics. The sought is not. as the Cartesians aver, hidden in an unreachable "out there," but rather in the searcher *in potentiae*. This is the constant mes-sage of the esoteric tradition, whether expressed in mystical, religious, or literary language.

Gnosiology of Romanticism

Putting this book into context with the dominant culture of the present world is no doubt a drier experience than I hope explor-ing its chapters will be. But it must be done. "The nineteenth century ended," says Huston Smith, "by swinging back to [Cartesian] Enlightenment predilections, and shunting off into literature and counter-enlightenment sentiments that had given rise to the Romantic Movement and German idealism. So philosophy entered the twentieth century allied to science."[11] It might be objected that a *gnosiology* of Romanticism cannot be concerned with the domestic affairs of philosophy as a discipline. Strictly speaking it cannot. But since nearly every adversary of mysticism and gnosis reproaches their practitioners with a lack of grounding in history and philosophy, the position of gnosiology in recent history must briefly be taken into account.

What the fate of modern philosophy seems to suggest is that the creative spirit, in effect what was "shunted off into literature," might well have kept the Western philosophical tradition alive had it stayed with philosophy as well as affecting literature. But as things turned out, it did not, and philosophy, having "allied with the sciences," later found itself in a crisis, realising that "autonomous reason, reason without infusions that both power and vector it, is helpless. By itself, reason can deliver nothing apodictic. Working (as it necessarily must) with variables, variables are all it can come up with." (Incidentally, this was precisely the recognition Coleridge made while writing his theory of Imagination and fancy: "fancy […] has no other counters to play with, but fixities and definites.") "The Enlightenment's natural light of reason turns out to have been a myth. Reason is not itself a light. It is more than a conductor, for it does more than transmit. It seems to resemble an adapter which makes useful translations, but on condition that it is powered by a generator."[12] If it is true that we have seen the end of Western philosophy, it is because its real generator, Imagination, was never acknowledged.

In many modern writings about Romanticism we are faced with a curious double-bind arising from the situation just described. Romanticism and its counter-enlightenment tendencies

---

are judged from criteria raised by science, and in a context "allied to science." The judgements passed by the academics on what is thinkable and unthinkable still arise from a complex of points of view which has, in the view of at least one contemporary, "played out its destiny and reached a dead end."[13] The very spark that might have kept philosophy alive lost the ears of a cultural community which now—increasingly obsessed with political, economic, and linguistic criteria— judges that the arts and literature are a mere epiphenomenon of the historical fabric. This is highly ironic as the story of a culture. The very literature into which the life-blood of philosophy was "shunted" is now disposed of according to a dead philosophy. The Romantic sentiment, the counter-enlightenment sentiment, is lost to view in materialism. Even the train metaphor, with which the philosopher chose to personify the late nineteenth century, is eerily appropriate to its Cartesian mentality, and inimical to the Romantic.

But now, again perhaps ironically, there is a chance for the new to enter, in the wake this time of the contemporary passion for deconstruction. All Western perspectives and modes of thought are now totally open for review, owing to the determined action of this analytical tool. Materialism's foundations have become as shaky as all the other ideologies hitherto deconstructed. Materialism is arguably as dead as all the ideas which it pronounced to be dead during the period of its dominance. If materialist philosophy is out, as it is according to Richard Rorty and Jacques Derrida, and if "conversation" and "play" are in, it still remains to ask what the matter for conversation will be. In the words of David Bohm, "just to talk, you must have some understanding of what order is and what meaning is."[14] If there is any message for the hardened academic in these essays on Romanticism, it may be to suggest new matters for the conversation which, bad weather notwithstanding, appears still to be going on. Further in preface I cannot go, save to say that the method of the writings I have found most compelling, like the practice of the spiritual hermeneutic circle, is best known and understood "by means of itself."[15] What the following essays aim at is to deepen our understanding of the "infusions that power and vector" reason, infusions that were present in uncommonly strong concentrations in the poetry of the Romantic era. In this sense, then, this is a book about Romanticism, but it is equally a study of the nature of the creative principle in the eyes of poets and mystics, and its role in the present and future of this culture.

It is widely known and taught in schools and universities that there were Romantic literary traditions of liberation, renewal, and of ideal forms of perception, sensation, cognition, of which the visionary as much as the visual is an important element. But nearly always, the relevance and most interesting implications of these very things are left unexplored. The purpose of these essays is to show that these impulses in Romanticism were far more than a literary tradition at the best of times, and that they certainly predated Romanticism by many centuries. Perhaps from pondering the depth and extent of the esoteric tradition—which the Romantics reinterpreted for modern western Europe—we shall see that it would be mistaken (as many studies have been, owing to the limitations of their premise) to ascribe the elements and signs of this tradition to one literary movement, or to one ideology or one world region. Romanticism had a physically small province (Europe) and historically a short one (a century); but to identify its province with its provenance is surely to provincialise—to diminish—our understanding of much more basic and essential principles. One of them is the question of what or who it is that grants in the first place the capacity to speculate or decide on what the meaning of Romanticism was, is, or might be.

———

1

THE QUESTION

—We are conductors perhaps of a creative intelligence.
—Yes. We may feel there is something in us, and we may
ask questions to bring it out.... The new idea was already
in the question. You can ask, where does the facility to be
aware of the questions come from, and perhaps that's the
nature of awareness.

—DAVID BOHM in conversation

THE CULTURE AND ART OF ROMANTICISM is studied for
many reasons, but every reader of its poetry, whether or not
the aim is to find it, will come to Wordsworth's question:

> Whither is fled the visionary gleam?
> Where is it now, the glory and the dream?[1]

Here, it might be said, is the question of questions. It is a question
arising in a multitude of forms that runs the gamut from questions shielding and yet revealing the real one—qualified questions such as Coleridge's, "Why do I always hurry away from any
interesting thought to do something uninteresting?" or "I want to
make a pilgrimage to the deserts of Arabia to find the man who
could make me understand how the one can be many"[2]—to the
more uncompromising inquiry: "What is life?" "Who is existing?"
"Who am I?"[3]

The question about questions, as Dom Sylvester Houédard
has called it, is perhaps always avoided until all the readily
answerable questions have been addressed. The political movements of Romanticism are exhaustively documented. So is the
psychology to a great extent. Studies of this type are readily

available. But the question still asked when the others are answered is the interesting one. It is all too easy to leave, as Coleridge reproaches himself for doing, in pursuit of "something uninteresting." It is the most difficult, because it is unique. It is the request for an answer beyond the answers offered by the fields of competence which all the Romantics, and their critics after them, have been educated in. This is why it is the question about questions: the question which makes all other questions possible, which is prior to, and in a sense unlike, *any* other question.[4] It is a question to which no amount of information, nor analysis, can be the answer. "Intellectual pretexts are for the loveless."[5]

Who am I? is one form the question takes. This occurs equally in all fields of human inquiry: in philosophy, depth pyschology, transactional analysis; as in creative writing, fiction, poetry; as in the manuals and teachings of mysticism.

The careers of the Romantic poets discussed in this book were marked by the variety of interests they pursued, religion, science, philosophy, and travel being amongst them. They were not simply "career" poets, interested only in verse form, the intricacies of meter, or the byways of classical reference and medieval allegory. Their poetry has been remembered amongst poetry readers, but that fact is only the slimmest—if still one of the most efficacious—of indicators as to the dynamics of their authors' inner and outer pursuits. Their real field was immense, larger than the genre "literary studies" could possibly indicate. The *manner* in which their various pursuits were conducted—alternately ecstatic and contemplative—suggests more about the nature of their search than do the genres its outcome came to occupy. Contemplation is more characteristic of the Romantic spirit than formal considerations like verse structure, or historical ones such as the French Revolution, or psychological biographical ones such as the impact on Shelley's work of his father-in-law.[6] It is not that these matters are irrelevant, far from it. But if they are taken to be the real reason why Romantic writers have commanded such widespread interest and admiration, then we are saying no more than that they lived much the same kind of life as many who did not become so canonized. Everyone is more—or less—involved in the historical, political, psychological, and social matter of their age, and *mutatis mutandis* all are alike in that involvement. But when it comes to the Romantics' equally celebrated moves toward the transcendent—that is, toward transcending, in knowledge and experience, the psycho-socio-political environment—we find something quite different: a statement of a priority for a certain type or state of being, made from a level which does not cast out the relevance of the environmental conditions, but which is not limited by those conditions either. A type of experience which, when addressed with a question, does not yield an answer confined to the life the questioner is stuck in, but rather an answer which changes, potentially throughout, the way that that life is experienced. Psychokinesis (meant here in J. G. Bennett's sense of ability to co-operate with the action of creative energy), the transformative experience,[7] changes the level *between* the moment of asking and the moment of hearing the reply.

We are really speaking here of a request to approach the level of the ultimate.[8] That is what I suggest underlies the constant searching, based in the question about questions, in which these poets engaged. Their other concerns could well have been addressed, and often were, by involvement and activity at the level demanded by the social, psychological, and political milieu, which is undoubtedly the way most people whose questions are asked at that level respond to them. But the contemplative/ecstatic nature of the Romantics' addresses to their world has its roots in something else: the suspicion that the outward problems of life are not answered at their own level, unless engagement with them is infused from a higher level with what may be called—with caution for the limitations of all these descriptions—the grounding power, creative energy, psychokinesis, inspiration, perfectible potential.

It is actually from this higher level that the Question about Questions really comes.[9] What is the meaning of meaning? The potential of possibility? The aim of pursuit? The significance of speech? Why create at all? The question about questions is also and inevitably the question about reality. The question about reality can be asked in thousands of ways, depending on its situation, but what distinguishes it is that it is not a question of "How do I survive?" or "How can I escape?" or "How can I win this game?" or "How do I protect my sense of self?" *The* question goes further than all those questions, and others too, questions, say, about justice, mental health, or satisfying "humanitarian needs." It is not unrelated to these, and certainly it is not a matter of hanging aloof from the human world; but the real question only arrives from a place beyond it, where something has been seen which may possibly have positive effects on the social order which the asker in his world is part of. But that amelioration is certainly not the sole aim in view when the askers of the question about questions open themselves by asking it. They are asking about the meaning of existence as such, first, and only next about existence as mirrored in their "own" existence. Only this question will bring responses that go further than the limited and relatively meaningless explanations that, on their own terms, economics, politics, and the natural sciences of the age could give. It is put well by Elémire Zolla, who suggests the value of repeating the questions "Who am I?" "What is I?"

> This might lead to the realization that personal identity is an illusion, that one is not one but many, until at last nonpersonal awareness, a witnessing anonymous centre, is firmly established; a non personal identity which is cosmic,

sheer being. If this is not achieved what difference does it make that it is you or somebody else, with another name, that goes through your body's mechanical set of motions? They are the result of social myths, conditionings you have never even inquired about.[10]

And the poets who asked the question of *whence and whither I?* seemed to know the state of consciousness in which this question, when asked, does not dissolve into thin air without return of any kind, but rather finds its point of contact. This state is the one about which perhaps half the poems in existence, only a small fraction of them "Romantic" poems, have been written; a state most often described as having been lost[11]—this being one way in which language seeks to amend its own inadequacy to the matter which the ultimate question addresses—a matter once known, but lost at the time the asker asks the question and opens himself. Only the "closed" can open; only the "lost" can be found, only the "separated" can reunite. "A new logic is suggested," says Dom Sylvester Houédard, "whereby the objections to tautology are abrogated, a logic whereby we see the truth of the proposition that 'Nothing can be what it is unless it is at the same time what it is not.'"[12]

We can equally well speak of the mysteries, or the Great Mystery, as we can of the Question of Reality. As the saying goes, "one mystery remains unsolved": it is indeed the nature of mystery to be the last remaining question, not answered by the manners and models of living encompassed by the "humanistic infrastructure": economics, emotions, ambitions, relationships.

It is important to remember that the false glamour connoted by terms like the Mysteries is not their substance but an accident of naming and of culture, strictly speaking, an irrelevance. It could be said that connotation *per se* is the history of accreted adventitious glamour on meaning that is already self-sufficient. The variety of existing terms for these levels in which the ultimate is approached is thus, from another point of view, a very useful fact, since the outworn terms and unfashionable references, even if their essence is understood, can be dropped, and new ones found which are less likely to provoke opposition or fall foul of prejudice.

An approach to the mystery of the Unanswered Question—the title given to Charles Ives' musical (and Bernstein's verbal) enunciation of it—is held to be possible, even though it is often held to be so by those whose written words, like Coleridge's, Shelley's, and Wordsworth's, seem as often to lament its loss as affirm its presence. But to disqualify the approach merely because it is adverted to in terms of loss is to limit oneself to the binary judgments of a world that we are trying to transcend or, more realistically, trying to understand from a place that has transcended it. It is in this sense that the play of imagination is indeed unlimited. For it is only through the imagination that that place subsists. A lower world can be accepted from the place of a higher, when the unlimited and unlimiting imagination is entered into. To disqualify as failure the expression of the lost state is to blind oneself to the essential reciprocity of losing and finding[13] whose avenue to a new post-dyadic logic we have just referred. The finding is not the only aim, as we shall see in the coming chapters. Losing is quite as much a part of it.

> [...] I have lost
> Beauties and feelings such as would have been
> Most sweet to my remembrance even when age
> Had diminished mine eyes to blindness!

> [...] now afflictions bow me down to earth:
> Nor care I that they rob me of my mirth;
>   But oh! each visitation
> Suspends what nature gave me at my birth,
>   My shaping spirit of Imagination.
>   (Coleridge, "Dejection Ode")

One of the reasons why the poetic principle itself, rather than its applications, engrossed all the Romantic artists and in a sense drew them together as a movement is that the experience of this principle opens us to the manifold levels of meaning that can be reached by language. Such opening is possible, however, only when language is used, and viewed, in a certain way. The poetic principle is fundamentally opposed to the principle of so-called direct description. The latter is said to be the main function of language, but it is actually no more than "the use of words to establish patterns of thinking whereby mankind is kept at a certain stage of ineptitude, or made to serve organisms which are ultimately not of evolutionary value."[14] That formulation, anonymously quoted from a Sufi master, makes the same point as the cautionary propositions put forward by Shelley in his *Defence of Poetry,* and Coleridge's remark in his essay on Imagination: "Rather ponder on why the ordinary man suffers from the tyranny of words, immobilized by custom until they only serve as tools." Coleridge intimates precisely the same with his famous phrase "the lethargy of custom." Compare Elémire Zolla: "In dealing with the intermediary world, only poetry will prevent symbols from turning into signs, nudges into definitions, living life into lived life"[15] or, in the words of Martin Notcutt, turning "self-knowledge into shelf-knowledge."[16]

Everything is interrelated. The effect that our thinking patterns have on our world-picture affects in turn the courage with which we can ask the great question, and possibly hear, or else not hear, the answers. What we find is that at its fullest power to amplify meanings, poetic language can relate the empirical biological life-theory with the next worlds, the world of the psyche being one of them, and one of the next called by the Persians the "world of seminal reasons."[17] The seminal and its process, germination, come to have a manifold meaning here, one physical, another metaphysical, with many intermediate levels.[18]

It is knowledge and experience of these levels and of moving between them, instead of a state of being fixed and habituated by "custom" at one level, which the varying interests of the Romantics pointed to. Such preoccupations as Shelley's with electrical shocks, ghosts, and the transformation of energies evident in alchemical symbolism;[19] such interests as Coleridge's in reverie and his experiments with hallucinogens; Wordsworth's pondering an emancipation from the habitual order of time—all point to something far wider than the practice of a literary craft, what may have been called the world of letters. Wordsworth said "Poets do not write for poets alone, but for men!" The very scope of their attention points to a much larger question than that of how to be a successful writer, or even how to write good poems. The Romantic movement, its projects, were concerned with the expansion of awareness, and the possibilities for the human being and human future opened up by an experience of that kind of expansion. It has often been called an activity of religion, philosophy, aesthetics, but in so naming it we find that the very limitations these poet-figures sought to free themselves from are reimposed. If it is seen, on the other hand, as an esoteric activity, then the picture changes. It is vital to remember that if we are to conceive of a level from which the Question about questions can be asked and the response heard, we must abandon our totemised faith in the superiority of the intellectual. From the point of view of the next dimension, in which Imagination is active, as Coleridge relates,[20] intellectual work is on an equal footing with book-keeping, moving earth, or rearranging furniture. It has no value above its contingent function. Just as, according to the Romantics, the classifying faculty—the finding of a category for everything in order to consider its significance known and valued—is the legacy of the intellectual faculty, so there is a great need to broaden the means of research into human possibility beyond the use of the intellect or rationalizing faculty alone. (Its prevalence has been attributed to the principles of the Greek language having been imposed on the entirety of human experience; a process which must inevitably restrict our breadth of competence.)[21] This need to broaden the repertoire of faculties probably accounts for the Romantics' privileging of a far wider field of inquiry than could be undertaken in the manner-bound belles-lettres, poetry, and fiction of the 18th century.

As far as current world views were concerned, the Romantic writers were well versed in the Aristotelian and the natural-scientific, and neither of these systems seemed to meet their question. The one possibility lay in looking for a way of transforming the very nature of their perception, their looking, speaking, asking; a change of consciousness that could not only be known of, known about, but known directly. Not by touch or taste alone, however. Access to this change of consciousness involved opening oneself to a direct metaphysical experience, in which the amplitude of the senses inner and outer is greatly increased, or in which, as the pursuit of reverie proved to Wordsworth, Coleridge, and Shelley, the certainty is reached that we live in more than one world at once and that when habitual awareness is breached for a moment and in abeyance, one lives in the next world and returns to the everyday world in a different "configuration" or state.[22] Owen Barfield saw in experience of the Imaginative World the bringing about of a "felt change of consciousness,"[23] a change which directed his own attention and studies from the time it happened (1923) to the present. It is this sense of *realized* change of being which gave Shelley such a strong conviction that poetry was involved with more than penmanship or elegance of formal execution, rather with a state where "the film of familiarity" is removed from awareness and another sight is opened. Like the Akasha, "It stands forever unmoved amid the moving and yet it moves with a speed infinitely beyond that of light."[24]

And what is that most brief and bright delight
Which rushes through the touch and through the sight,
And stands before the spirit's inmost throne
A naked seraph? None has ever known.

(Shelley)[25]

But might he, in creativity, come to know? Dom Sylvester Houédard raises this same unknowability: "The basic question will be basic only if there is no answer to it: It will establish the distinction between problems as questions that can be answered and mystery as *that question* that makes all other questions possible and is thus unique and unlike any other question."[26]

A human being's very existence is a question, in that it is constant flux, or becoming, and the question here consists in asking what is it that directs or impels this change in a manner that is meaningful rather than a habituated case of more of the same? What is seen as static, as duration, or as being the case, is actually merely a flash or instant in what (seen differently) is a constant process of change, what Coleridge called "the *lichtpunct* [sic] in the indivisible undivided duration."[27] What we find at the root of any question is a being attracted, drawn by what is unknown toward a state which will move the potential knower, whose possibility of knowing is constantly developing, closer to the sought. What attracts is, as yet, in the unknown, and its power to attract is the mover of time, the agent of the flux which we commonly see as linear time, life, the biographic journey.[28]

The hiddenness of the power to attract gives us some insight into the mystery so frequently alluded to by the Romantic poets, a mystery which is beyond conceptualisation, outside time (because it is initiating time itself into the existences we think it has, drawing it into birth) and referred to in terms of the far shore, the other side; the beyond; the aim of flight; that in relation to which earth is a stranger and at the same time a reflection.

If *this question that we are* is what human beingness is, then
the questions that it makes possible will all be ultimately
questions about being, about what *we are particular and
concrete examples of.*[29]

writes Sylvester Houédard, echoing Coleridge's question
about the wise man in the Arabian desert who may illuminate
the matter of how "one can be many"; and continuing:

It means asking not only why we are but how we are part
of it and how we know we are part of it, and so ultimately
we ask also about the value and limits of human knowledge, whether as knowledge of the question or as knowledge of the answer.[30]

That the poets were especially qualified to address this question was suggested long ago by the Sufi metaphysician and
poet Ibn 'Arabi: "One in whom the Active Imagination is not
at work will never penetrate to the heart of the question."[31]
These are matters which not only poetry and the other arts,
but also science, philosophy, and religion are all concerned
with. When Wordsworth said "Poetry is the breath and finer
spirit of all knowledge," he meant it. For him, poetry was an
attitude to living (and dying), not a literary escape from it as
many later critics would have us believe. What the diversity of
the Romantics' interests—their search beyond mere success
in the writer's craft—points us to is the need to find a universal medium with which to mention and pursue the question
about questions; a language, as well as a way of life, capable of
dismantling the barriers with which one discipline seems, in
our narrowed world, to exclude the co-operation of another;
and an attitude of seeking which allows the greatest possible
scope of receptivity. Shelley claimed for poetry that it is "at
once the root and blossom of all other systems of thought."

The implications of this startling proposition are opened up by comparing the Romantics' views about poetry with the esoteric tradition's accounts of human existence.

The question about questions is also the best kind of prayer as well as the best kind of poetry, in that it is the direct invitation, or invocation, of the creative principle. What Shelley desired in the *Defence of Poetry*, a reunion of the scientific and the religious impulse, enabled by understanding that creativity is the source of both, is a goal rapidly being neared in the explorations of the new physics and of ecology, and their parallels with the metaphysical languages of other cultures, for example Tibetan Buddhism.

2

SACRED GRAMMAR

Toward a Mystical Structuralism

They told me I was everything: 'tis a lie.

—SHAKESPEARE, *King Lear*

TO BELIEVE THAT ROMANTICISM was the cult of personal genius is an error. The orthodoxy that describes Romanticism this way turned off onto a wrong road before the journey of interpretation was as much as begun. Many theories on the Romantics privilege the self, the individual, invoking Shelley's and Byron's adventures as an unprecedented indulgence of the ideal of self. So scholars are sometimes content with generalizations such as:

> Idealistic philosophy progresses from the basis of classical ontology to the discovery of the human personality at the center of all knowledge and action.[1]

Whether from the rationalist or the idealist point of view, there has been handed down a mythos or culture known as the humanities, which is the cornerstone of modern democratic politics, of most psychology, certainly of what is known as the Western liberal education. From it derive the now sacrosanct notions of the "rights of man" (and of woman).

But there is a question which this familiar etiology of civilization (which we have come to regard as truth) did not pause to ask in its construction of history, let alone answer. That is, what is the *nature* of the self, individual, subject, personality, call it what you will, which is so much in the foreground? What is its guarantee, if any? If we look at the external documentation, we find that it is an entity taken for granted. The only generation or sector of people for whom it was not taken for granted were the mystics, poets, and gnostics, and in our own age, the post-structuralists. We could agree that as far as concerns history and the political order, the individual is the product of a system of conditioning which has survived on the basis of enlightened self-interest, and has been worked into a multitude of constructions which take highly complex names, determinations, and sublimations; thence we extrapolate culture, high culture, and aesthetics. Religion is also of this order. Game theory has suggested the elaboration of patterns of self but rarely the *raison d'être* of these, let alone their provenance.

The poets and mystics investigate the generation of these patterns more deeply than the philosophy of deconstruction has managed to do. Deconstruction starts from predicating the self or subject on language. Materialist philosophy, accepting language as a gestural code, tacitly complies with this predication, and rationalises the Romantic exaltation of the individual on this basis, occasionally reproaching it for bearing totalitarian overtones. It concludes, like deconstruction, by saying that the glorious Romantic subject was a construct like all the other constructions of human identity, which put the human personality in the center.

If we turn to the poets' own writings on the subject of self, identity, and language, I believe we come to something very different from what "received wisdom" offers us in the way of evidence for the Romantics' view of the human self. Shelley:

How vain it is to suppose that words can reveal to us the mystery of our being. Rightly used they can make evident our ignorance to ourselves, and this is much.[2]

Coleridge, writing of "existence in and by itself," says:

> … least of all may we hope to find its origin, or sufficient
> cause, in the moulds and mechanisms of the understand-
> ing, the whole purport and function of which consist in
> individualisation, in outlines, and differencings by quan-
> tity, quality and relation […] We have asked then for
> [existence's] birth-place in all that constitutes our relative
> individuality, in all that each man calls exclusively himself.
> It is an alien of which they know not: and for them the
> question itself is purposeless, and the very words that con-
> vey it are as sounds in an unknown language....[3]

It's obvious that the "relative individuality" (the "Western-
ised subject" of the deconstructionist) was even at this stage
fully acknowledged to be unable to penetrate to the question,
what we called in the previous chapter "the question about
questions." While Shelley speaks of ignorance as the only
reward of linguistic structuring, Coleridge speaks of a foreign
language and alien country. As far as the self is concerned, it
is certain that for Coleridge and Shelley here the mystery is
the matter; it is the destination of questions that they not only
ask in language, the language of their acculturation, humanistic or otherwise, but also ask in their being, a question their
whole lives could be said to be given to asking. Lives spent not
in glorification of the personality but rather given to seeking
behind the spectre of personality to the mystery beyond it—
the essence, as Gurdjieff put it, which conditioning masks;
which meditation unmasks; the essence which false personality, occasionally fading, reveals in its unbidden, unexpected
radiance.

"That it is, and affirms itself to be, is its only predicate," says
Coleridge of this existence which seized "the nobler among
men," the "elect" (feeling "in themselves something ineffably

greater than their own nature") with "a sort of sacred horror."[4] The kind of experience he speaks of, far from glorifying the internal personality, moved to annihilate it. Hence the horror, and the recognized inadequacy of the cultivated tools of civilization, language, and reason, to come to an understanding of it.

"That it is, and affirms itself to be, is its only predicate."[5] Coleridge was obviously aware of the potentially absolute relation of being and language, and that philosophical uses of language, even specially esoteric uses, were just as involved in the "science of Being" as science was. It is here, along with the mystics and, paradoxically, the structuralists, that the poets encounter the sheerness of Being in itself, but encounter it as speakers, as selves who feel called to give an account of the ineffable, or "to eff the ineffable" as Samuel Beckett, in his own German Romantic period, put it.

If our "ignorance is made clear to ourselves" by our language, as Shelley suggests, then the question arises, who is the self to whom language makes such ignorance clear? If it is an ignorant self, can it have anything made clear to it? The answer may be no, ignorances are not clarities. Or it may be yes, in that only the non-delimited can be totally transparent.

If the tool we use—language—only makes clear our ignorance, then it follows that the self we took for granted as a competent agent to use it to uncover the mystery of our being is not competent at all. Instead of a self, with its accumulated rights, and its accustomed qualities, preferences, and aversions, it is revealed to be an empty space, a *clear ignorance.* Self's business, its quest for new sensations, its sense of continuity and importance, is merely evading—trying to deny—its own real emptiness: rather like the pornographer's camera, the self is never content.

Shelley says, however, that to recognize the reality of ignorance precisely where a competent self was presumed to subsist, "is much." "Rightly used, [words] can make evident our ignorance to ourselves." We can agree and add that it is the starting point of a knowledge which only makes itself evident to a person, in W.B. Yeats's words, "from whom has fallen all even of personal characteristic."[6] Thomas Merton explains how a human *survives* the falling-away of his presumed identity:

> The ego-subject [...] instead of being realized in its own limited self-hood is spoken of rather as simply vanishing out of the picture altogether. [It] is not that the person loses his metaphysical or even physical status, or regresses into non-identity, but rather that his *real* status is quite other than what appears empirically to be his status.[7]

Experiencing such a reversal of perspective, this "vanishing out of the picture," is exactly what gives rise to the "sacred horror" which Coleridge speaks of as overtaking the prophets and gnostics. They recognize then that it is precisely not the "personal characteristic" or "relative individuality" which reaches or knows the mystery of being, but another knower to whom the word *reality* is actually more appropriate than it is to the empirical self. An *event* of knowing is definitely said and felt to happen, otherwise it would not be possible to notice, as Shelley does, the revelation of one's ignorance so as to say "this is much." And it is to this event of knowing that Coleridge, Blake, and Shelley, along with the Buddhists, Taoists, Vedantists, and Sufis, were repeatedly and constantly committing their efforts. We cannot quite say committing them*selves*, because in their severest gnostic eventualities, their empirical self was only the vehicle, not the impetus. This is hinted at, and its motivation even more subtly intimated, when Coleridge speaks in the "Dejection Ode" of the "inanimate cold world allowed" to the "ever-anxious, loveless crowd." More is said on this in another chapter but suffice it to say here that

---

the "over-protective anxiety for one's supposed self and its sake" is precisely what kills the world and its anima/animation; and that the action of love at once enlivens, warms the world—indeed *allows* it in a deeper sense—and annihilates the anxious self whose defining characteristic is love*less*ness. So when the mystic with Yeats speaks of a longing for a soul-state from which "has fallen all even of personal characteristic except thirst for that hour when all this shall pass away like a cloud," he does not mean it as the pessimist materialist might mean it, but means it in the sense of the "ending of time,"[8] the event of crossing into the next world where the conditions of time and space do not apply in the same way as they do in the first world. Blake refers to this "ending of time" when he says:

> whenever any Individual Rejects Error and Embraces Truth, then a Last Judgement passes upon that Individual.

> Error, or Creation, will be burned up, & then, & not till then, will Truth or Eternity appear. It is burnt up the moment Men cease to behold it.[9]

Such a transformation of the person, represented by this experience of the "ending of time," "last judgement," "passing away of personal characteristic," called the Sufi death, or annihilation of laws, actions, attributes, and essence,[10] is ultimately the very allower of love. No gargantuan self-aggrandizement such as was envisaged for the Romantics by their materialist critics could have profited the planet for one moment. For all the poets, including Keats, the meaning of love was not to be found in pursuing the established satisfactions of the relative individuality, nor in the exhortations of conventional religion, which in addressing the fear for safety of human beings still only addresses their relative individuality, not that which their individuality was meant to exemplify, which is something very different. The poets sought the originary meaning of love in the states where the individual as constructed, far from fulfilling its desires, could only collapse, disappear, and another action be perceived beginning to work. Crucial to the meaning of this self-annihilation was that it was the sole condition for the making apparent of love as a positive force. "Whoever loses his life shall find it" is how the writer of the Gospel experiences this. Whoever loses the limited personality finds the real life of this world, real only in that it comes from the higher worlds into this, through the action of those whose selves are seen to be what they are, that is, contingencies for the expression and flowing-out of necessary being, "existence without analogon" which, "being limitless, comprehending its own limits in its dilatation, and condensing itself into its own apparent mounds, how shall we name it?"[11] It would be easy to mistake these words of Coleridge's for an extract of a Tibetan Buddhist text, their exercise being so similar.

It may seem that this is an odd place for a discussion to go which started with the poets declaring that language could not be used as a tool to uncover the real mystery of being. But in Coleridge's and Blake's repeated invitations to recognize the self-annihilating properties of language, coupled with their interest in the source of the I-particle with which the relative individuality speaks of its so-called self, there is an extraordinary indication by following which readers of the Romantics can bypass the blind alley of rationalist thought and arrive at a point where the ancient mystics and twentieth century deconstructionists, perhaps unbeknownst to one another, actually meet. Or at least gaze across a gulf and see one another. For the Rationalist understanding of culture depends for its validity precisely on a self which the mystics in their work, and the poststructuralists in theirs, have declared to be non-existent. We could say that the liberal-humanist view of history, still animating our political and social assumptions from top to bottom, is "based" on an unreality. If it is so, then the "ritual absurdity" which modernism and the counterculture have forced us to acknowledge is no surprise, but simply the unreal self attempting to build where, and what, it cannot.

To investigate this matter we must move from the large frame of history to the small frame of syntax, grammar, and parts of speech as they are used by the artists of the imagination. Language and being reflect one another. We can say that language polarizes being in the same way as relative polarizes absolute. One of the staples of such polarized language is THIS and THAT.[12] The two words make it possible to point to multiplicity. At the same time we can say, echoing a Sanskrit phrase, that THAT is the first existence, and THIS is the relative, or entification of THAT. Or, more schematically,

THAT is the absolute of which the relative is THIS.

This order can be pursued further in the following remark:

> Images "stand in" to represent what is in fact unknowable, non-ceptual and non-evidential to us, who are negatively situated on this side of consciousness. Such images can only be real in themselves, however, in so far as they represent, or re-present, the eternal reality of THAT. When they become real in themselves, then we are only over-stating them and have become *idolaters* guilty of the error of the Sanskrit word *upadhi*, which is treating THAT as if it is only this, and so confusing the lesser with the greater.[13]

If we now remind ourselves of the non-duality of *that*, which Shelley, following the Platonists, calls the one, and Coleridge "Existence in and by itself, without analogon," we come to contemplate the referent of a series of characterisations of the Uniqueness.

Tat tvam asi (That I am)

(*Upanishads*)[14]

In the beginning was the Word, and the Word was with God. And the Word was God.

(St. John 1: 112)

THAT was the frame of reference for the Druids, which is what makes them so different from our experience now, which is determined, not by the truth of THAT, but by our anxious need for more security, more gain, less loss, and more power over the other.

(E.G. Howe)[15]

Unity as a word should be the most comprehensive word, the omnicomprehensive word, *the* word. Applied to the beginning of the Gospel of St. John, this identification makes metaphysical sense of the prologue. Replace *word* or *logos* with *oneness* and the text opens up.

(Zolla)[16]

The mysterious source whose being is knowledge, whose knowledge is being, the adorable I AM IN THAT I AM.

The eternal act of creation in the infinite I AM, the great I AM, and [...] the filial word that re-affirmeth it from eternity to eternity, whose choral echo is the universe.

(Coleridge)[17]

...having a writing tablet and taking account of the numbers who arise, is that Angel of the Divine Presence mentioned in Exodus XIV C., 19v and in other places: [...] called by the Name of Jehovah Elohim, the "I AM" of the oaks of Albion.

(Blake)[18]

———

We can say that just as creation is the "dualitude"[19] of an original unity, so language is the refraction into parts of what is in principle a whole, the first person singular.

In the ancient language structure which this list of statements exemplifies, the only person qualified to use the first person singular is God, Deity, or Source—this as much in the Hindu as in the Hebrew world; so that it is understandable why certain divine names are forbidden from being uttered by people. This fact interested Coleridge, as can be seen by his repeated invocation, over all periods of his life, of the tetragrammaton which equals the Sanskrit *tat tvam asi* (I am that I am). This is the non-duality which is the necessary condition for all multiplicity, duality included.

It is impossible for language to speak of the non-duality because language is sequential and the unity as unity is prior to sequence. Just as the source is prior to the outflowing of water, this *sequence* only starts to happen in what is called the divine *devolutions*, and thus we have terms such as the path of return, descent, ascent, creations, manifestations, and so on. Language, being an evolutionary-devolutionary medium, very rarely fails to perpetrate its own devolutions and multiplications. As language is a minister of distinguishing and entifying, that is all as it has to be. But it means that *language only moves close to the Unity when its sequencing function is frustrated and it collapses, closes in on itself.* Then and only then does it reveal essentially the nullity of its other functions as far as penetrating the mystery of being is concerned. As the school of Ibn 'Arabi put it, "the intellect [...] is that which, on a cognitive level, restricts the non-restricted and delimits the non-defined. Hence it is barred from grasping the ultimate origin of things—non-delimited Being—through its own powers."[20]

The function of language abandoning its sequentiality, and its correlative being-state, has been called the hypostatic dimension of unity, as opposed to its devolution in manifestation from which derive the metaphysical images of the journey, the love affair, homesickness,[21] the four Worlds, and the Dialogues (themes explored throughout the rest of this book). The Hypostatic dimension is illustrated in a collapse of language for which the texts of the Taoists and Buddhists could be said to be the prime example, and theosophy to be the contrary (that is, the ramification of the unity in principles and orders).

The collapse of language, in the world we know, comes halfway between the effort or enterprise of explanation and a hearing of the silence of the ultimate. But since it is a collapse-point, what one could call a crisis in the first world, it bears strong comparison to the moment of entry from the first world into the imaginal world, described in Chapter 5.

Some forms, all of them severe, taken by this collapse are present in Taoist formulae and paradoxes such as:

> Change is the sole unchanging existent.
> The Tao that can be spoken is not the tao.
> The only security is that there is no security.

or Socrates:

> All I know is that I know nothing.

or Wittgenstein's somewhat different, but related, gnomon:

> That which one cannot speak of, one must be
> silent about.

Another variation is the set of proverbs relating to the supreme self in Hebrew, Islamic, and Gnostic traditions, which Coleridge and Blake were attracted to because they eventuate a literal collapse of predicate:[22]

EHYEH/JHVH
I am that I am
Tat tvam asi
La ilaha illa 'lah (There is no God but God).

According to these precepts all predications are, from the point of view of the ultimate, false and the seeker of the ultimate must recognize this (here precisely is the difference between the Sufis' "necessary being" and "contingent being"),[23] and since language in its sequenced or non-hypostatic mode is the language we know and use, words are futile, and the questioner ends up in silence, like the Buddhist in meditation or like Shelley's soul "pinnacled dim in the intense inane."[24] Such hypostatic language offers the opportunity to view that which is beyond words, not as a goal of sentimentalist escapism but rather as a discipline. It is what Andrew Harvey ventured to call a "technology," which recognizes what the uses are of the medium of sequential consciousness (the first world), and equally recognizes where those uses stop.

Perhaps the most significant matter to emerge here is the absolute priority of this hypostatic statement for the poet Coleridge, who saw it as the pinnacle, or fountain, or source, of his entire system of creative imagination and its functions in poetry and philosophy:

My faith is this: God is the Absolute will. It is his Name and the meaning of it. It is the hypostasis. As begetting its own Alterity, the Jehovah, the Manifested, he is the Father; but the love and the life—the spirit—proceeds from Both.[25]

Analysis of the hypostatic mention or word reveals the person, I, and the verb, AM, (BE).[26] Identity and existence are the first principles, then. One identity, one existence.

Elémire Zolla succeeds (where many have failed) in spelling it out:

> Of all verbs, only one can denote static unity; the one that is not of motion but of station: to be. Be in itself and by itself in the infinitive tense denotes timelessness: the One. To be on the one hand contains, on the other negates, whatever was, is, shall, or might be.
>
> As the copulation of past and present which is timelessness, symbolized in the vegetable and animal world by seeds, which contain both the past and the future, in language it is betokened by the copula of subject and predicate—the verb "be"....
>
> The word, then, is "Be." All words imply that they *be*, as all realities imply metaphysical experience.[27]

The verb *be*, then, is unique in language. It is the only verb which perfectly embodies "the engendering command." As Zolla also puts it:

> No word can speak the truth, but can only signify clusters of forms, images, dreams, with the one exception of Be [...] Apart from offering in "Be" the symbol of oneness, languages are nothing but textures of metaphors, of conveyances.[28]

In the hypostatic statement of unity, the cosmic I AM, there is no particularization; the only identity that can speak this is the identity of the unqualified.[29] And when we recognize that all the conveyances of the qualified are necessarily imbued with the Unqualified, we come to the esoteric meaning of the metaphysical conversation. "In reality there is no knowledge of God by another than God, for another than God there is not. [...] 'I am the mirror of thy face; through thine own eyes I look upon thy countenance.'"[30]

In the transition between the phrases "The Word was God" and "the Word was made flesh" we can intuit the incident of divine devolution, the apparency with which the hypostatic unity is shown to us on the side we see it from usually. It is a step from non-being to being, which we find according to the esoteric tradition is an event that happens in "no time at all." This continual recreation of reality at every moment, or in no time, is hidden in the proverb that suggests the Persian carpet will fly if you step on it at *precisely* 3 a.m. This time/no time is the lightning flash in which prophetic insights are communicated. And it is this kind of border-line between Being in Itself and Being subject to the engendering command "Be!," that is, Being as known in place and name, that is meant by the dissolution of self in inspiration and enlightenment. Zolla says:

> Only apart from one's shape and name can one reach truth. [...] What makes us real is our need to be a monad, which is impossible insofar as we coincide with our personal equation: our name and shape.[31]

By personal equation here is meant what humanism calls self, what deconstruction calls the subject.

Zolla continues:

> Absolute individuality and absolute universality coincide in the monad of metaphysical experience; this cannot be "touched" by "sober" words. Words as such are signifiers that cannot signify significance itself, what lies before, above, beneath the opposition of a signifier and a thing signified, of likeness and difference [...]

As the peak of metaphysical experience, of utter silence and unity, the meaning of all this is revealed, in the sense that, once reached, the need and quest for factual reality is seen through and ceases.

All that is not at this level is unreal, not reality-giving, according to Vedanta; it possesses being like the snake for which one has mistaken a rope—only by virtue of the rope and only so long as it is not discriminated from the rope.[32]

So, one may ask, if it is only apart from one's shape and name that one can reach this truth of absolute unity, what is the point of the world, the worlds, the words, images, dreams, characters, of which the poets and philosophers all speak? Are they not so much useless baggage? From one angle the answer is yes, they are. Thus Novalis, at his most terse:

$$I = Not\ I.[33]$$

and Shakespeare, saying the same:

> Nor I nor any man that but man is,
> With nothing shall be pleased till he be eas'd
> With being nothing.[34]

And Coleridge, returning yet again to the subject:

> Let a young man separate I from Me as far as he possibly can, and remove me till it is almost lost in the remote distance. "I am Me" is as bad a fault in intellectuals and morals as it is in grammar, whilst none but one—God—can say "I am I" or "That I am."[35]

When this has happened, then factual reality, personal identity, as object of question and need, ceases, in the light of

———

understanding that the quest is not for that. Neither was need itself intended for these objects which are, after illumination, realized to be contingent, not necessary. So the world is not left behind in some pseudo-ascetic mystical flight, and neither can the illuminated person simply become the target of moral judgment. He or she is, as the Sufis say, not of the world but still in it.[36] "One may live with a man in *samadhi* and never be aware of it. His spirited reaction to events can be mistaken for active participation and concern, his aloofness for torpor."[37] Similarly, the realization of union is not a to-be-wished-for state of attainment, nor actually an achievement, because it is not something which you are not already. The language of achieving and attaining is spoken and imagined in the world of time and space which, in the state of union, loses all claim to reality-status. Here, "whoever says *A* must not thereby say *B* and *Z*, on the contrary he has already said them. [...] thinking is autonomous [...] it is irresistible."[38]

The person for whom this transformation has happened is, as far as the judgments of the world are concerned, much as he or she was before. Whoever sees with the eye of the next world, with Blake's "eye of vision," or has a taste of that state, will know the difference. So the question is asked again: are not names, images, personalities, dreams, and thoughts the very stuff of the humanities and arts? Or are they no more than useless baggage from the gnostic's angle? The reply may be that once the annihilated identification with the baggage is effected in a human life, the names and determinations under which that person nevertheless lives are neither the goal of existence—the pride of one's life—nor the problem that the term *baggage* suggests they were or might be. For someone still in aversion to the world is still bound to it by the laws of attachment, which manifest in possessiveness or hate, like or dislike. But for someone for whom "all trace of charac-teristic [...] has fallen," the world's conditions will no longer be coveted prizes but only stand as indicators of *whence* this world is merely contingent.

The psychology of studying the celestial hierarchies or worlds, then, is not aimed at grasping the top and using it to exploit the bottom: that is the project which egalitarian thought fears. On the contrary, a recognition of the essential nature of *archy*, let us say holarchy or synarchy[39] if not hierarchy, simply sees everything in its place, so it is neither to be grasped at nor repudiated but simply faced and responded to as, in the moment of eternity, the auspicious moment, the *kairos*, it presents itself.

It is the difference between seeing the world from one side or from the other that gives rise to the endless debates, which are as rife in discussion of Shelley and Coleridge as in theology, about pantheism as opposed to monotheism.[40] These debates simply dissolve in the asking of the question about questions: Who is conscious? Who sees? Whose identity are we striving to protect? In the words of Rumi:

> There's no way a metaphor can say this. There is no true comparison. All images are hopelessly weak when it comes to saying
> > *You did not throw when you threw.*

> The God-knower cannot be fooled the same way twice.
> He's out of the hexagonal well,
> This up-and-down, left-right,
> Front-back container.[41]

The work of the German mystic Jacob Böhme, in whom Blake and Coleridge took such interest, changes the level at which language is seen to operate when self-annihilation has occurred. It becomes possible to perceive language working on another "harmonic,"[42] as it were.

———

Rather than language as the speech spoken by human beings, we are asked to contemplate the universe devolving from the Unqualified Source as the *word* spoken by that source, the entifying *I am* spoken by God, "whose choral echo" says Coleridge, "is the Universe." Böhme:

> [the] unitie with knowledge speaketh forth itself eternally onto an object: the word is the speaking or breathing of the will out of the power by the understanding: It is the driving and forming of the eternal power as to an infiniteness of multiplicitie, as the Creator of powers, out of the sole power [in vertue]...

> The word *wisdom* is the outflown word, as an object of the divine knowledge of divine will, as essential power of the great love of God; from whence all things have received their motion and possibilitie.

> The word JEHOVAH, is understood: the life of the Abyss, as of the Unity: therein is also understood the most holy name Jesus: as the egress'd I, as the ground and fountain of the breathing of God's Unitie.

> Everything has its mouth to manifestation: and this is the language of nature, whence everything speaks out of its property, and continually manifests, declares, sets forth itself.[43]

So the humanistic perspective is turned on its head when it is first asked, then finally realized, who is doing the speaking. If the universe *is* the eloquence of divine effusion, a point of departure shared by Christian, Islamic, Buddhist, and Vedantic esotericism, then the silencing of the self and its baggage opens the ears to the real speaker, the "supreme unhindered speech, the Brahma sound,"[44] whose "words" are Nature as well as the words spoken by humans. Thus we've returned, as every varied perspective on the matter will eventually do, to a metaphysical *conversation* which the poets and mystics are involved in. The word of reality, then, is best appreciated in silence, in the suspension of the clatter of personality represented by the so-called humanistic self. A different encounter takes place in this silence.

This is a grand shift of perspective, but our culture is constantly in danger of forgetting that it is a shift which does not depend on established religion to make. The example offered by the Romantics is ample demonstration.

3

THE METAPHYSICAL CONVERSATION

The Romantics and Meditation

All real living is meeting.

—MARTIN BUBER

The *cognitio matutina* is not only a contemplation of Eternal Ideas; it is encountering Archangels of Light. […] For the adept, "journeying in company with the Angel" is in a wholly different situation from the philosopher perfecting a theory of knowledge.

—HENRY CORBIN

THE INNER TRADITIONS open an unexpected perspective on the time-honored subject of the Romantic poets' interest in the surrounding world, and particularly in landscape. Again we must bear in mind that the phenomenon we are to explore is not confined to the part of cultural history called the Romantic period, but happens to find here an unusually even and concentrated distribution of examples. We can say that it is characteristic of Romanticism to that extent, but much more important, it is characteristic of all creative activity or receptivity as a matter of principle.

The way in which the Western consciousness is mostly educated conditions most of us into an assumption that the world is outside us, and that we are onlookers who alternately struggle with it, manipulate it, appreciate it, feel close to it, feel far from it, as the situation may decide. It may be pleasing, it may be repellent, more often than not it is neither, but in all contexts it is seen as other. This is, roughly speaking, the assumption which classical physics has inbred in our culture and which the philosophers of the seventeenth century and the Enlightenment (so-called) expressed as empirical Rationalism and materialism. Coleridge found that "Mind, in Newton's system, is always passive, a lazy looker-on on an external world."[1] As Ajahn Sumedho put it, speaking of the time before he became a Buddhist:

> Nature is something out there; it's what you see. There are mountains and trees, and there are natural laws, but they have very little to do with you, so you tend to feel like an alien.[2]

What is historically significant here is that these assumptions were current in a form that dominated most estimates of what was reality and what was illusion.[3] This, what philosophy called the "mind-body problem," meant that myth, dream, the psychic life, and religion, all simultaneously present to people's awareness, took on the status of illusion or unreality, and was consigned to the realm of diversion at best, nonsense at worst, by those known as the sceptics.[4] The very reputation of the sceptic could not have emerged in the absence of this dichotomy of values which purported the material world to be real and the rest of the multifarious contents of consciousness to be unreal. The sceptics, according to this state of conditioning, were the realists, and their opposites—idealists and believers— were the deluded ones.[5] This attitude is responsible still for the dyadic cast of mind which only feels safe once it has assigned reality to one class of propositions and experiences, and rejected the other class. A crucially divided number of judgements have, for example, centered around "paranormal" phenomena, where evidence is in such variety and conflict that swiftness to side either with the *pro* or *contra* argument is emphasized to the exclusion of methods normally known to be reliable guides. In face of evidence they admit they cannot refute, some scientists persist in refusing to contemplate what to any other field of research would be inevitable conclusions.[6] This is a scene in which superstition[7] appears in both camps; and the very existence of the camps no less than the tendency of superstition itself are symptoms of that dyadic thinking which keeps a controversy alive by constantly enthroning and dethroning ideas. Our culture, as Koestler remarked, has been "for two thousand years ensnared in the logical categories of Greek philosophy which permeate our vocabulary and concepts, and decide for us what is thinkable and what is unthinkable."[8] "Archetypes rotate all the time; as with the unconscious, when dealing with them, they are not to be manipulated. One must give up negation, dyadic thinking."[9]

The Romantics' remarkable characteristic is like the mystics'. In this dyadic model, it is the impulse toward liberation from confinement. The unthinkable and the thinkable are the two camps into which the thinkers batten themselves down and prepare to establish—or topple—one another's chiefs. But the state of contemplation is essentially prior to the establishing and evaluation of contraries; it offers another possibility, another question, and it does this in another mode.

There is no need to rehearse in exhaustive detail the instances in which Wordsworth, Keats, Coleridge, and Shelley refer to contemplation of landscape—this would amount to a list that has been made many times before. What we are exploring here is what the nature of such a contemplation is, what originated it, what it meant to them that it should become the focus of so many instances of mention. It goes far beyond simply "a feeling of pleasure" evoked from memories "recollected in tranquility."[10] These types of formulation, at which point so many discussions of Romantic poetry stop, have been current for so long that they grow stale with age—forms which Beckett called "mouldy old reliables ... a few usual flowers ... azure, that never dies."[11] They have grown so worn only because their meaning perhaps has still to penetrate, as to dissolve, the Western logical snare which Koestler identified as so entrenched. Even in stating *metaphysical experience* to be "a good designation for the effects of contemplation," Elémire Zolla is immediately aware of a danger: "it should be periodically checked, and replaced before it sounds hollow and shrill, before it is taken for granted."[12] The desuetude of a metaphor or image owes as much to the shortcomings of our receptivity, its lack of education, as it does to the wornness of the image.

It may be possible to come to a less hollow understanding of the Romantics' relation to landscape by considering these statements together:

(i) [The human] response to the beauty of landscape isn't a simple "objective" matter. Does a [person] partly make up what he sees and feels as a beautiful landscape out of what he is in himself—or out of a combination of what he is and what he aspires to be? I don't mean that he projects himself into the landscape. He attends with passionate interest to particular features that are really there. But as he does so, is he at the same time unconsciously seeking some more general perception and understanding of life and, in that, finding more of himself? [...] When he is thoroughly drawn out of himself, to attend to what is really there, the artist can hardly be fully conscious of why this is happening, and nor can we recognize at all promptly why we are attracted by the work he then creates. Together they distinguish this landscape from the [one] that is characterized by what Ruskin named the pathetic fallacy. Here the landscape is distorted, [...] only [...] contributing to the lyric or dramatic handling of

[an] emotion. The more secret appeal is made when a landscape is speaking to something deeper and more permanent than an emotion, giving us knowledge not of a state of feeling but of a state of being.[13]

(John Newton, 1975)

(ii) [...] The difference [...] between objective and subjective: A picture of Christ or Buddha is merely the record of something observed by a behaviorist and interpreted by a theologian. But when you're confronted with a landscape like this, it's psychologically impossible for you to look at it with the eyes of a J. B. Watson or the mind of a Thomas Aquinas. You're almost forced to submit to your immediate experience; you're practically compelled to perform an act of self-knowing [...]

"That's why we always hang this kind of painting in our meditation room."

"Always landscapes?"

"Almost always. Landscapes can really remind people of who they are."

"And do you meditate on this picture?" Will asked.

"Not *on* it. *From* it, if you see what I mean. Or rather parallel with it. I look at it, and other people look at it, and it reminds us all of who we are and what we aren't, and how what we aren't might turn into who we are.

The Clear Light comes first. You go mad about sunsets because sunsets remind you of what's always been going on, whether you knew it or not, inside your skull and outside space and time."[14]

(Huxley, *Island*)

(iii) In looking at objects of nature while I am thinking, as at yonder moon dim-glimmering through the dewy window-pane, I seem rather to be seeking, as it were *asking*

for, a symbolical language for something within me that already and forever exists, than observing anything new. Even when the latter is the case, yet still I have always an obscure feeling as if that new phenomena [sic] were the dim awakening of a forgotten or hidden truth of my inner nature.[15]

(Coleridge, *Anima Poetae*, 1805)

(iv) The mountain first lightened up by the rays of the dawn also enlightens the intelligence, since dawn and intelligence are one.[16]

(*Zend Avesta*)

(v) There is a coincidence between dawn's breaking and the awakening of one's self ... Rising dawn and awakening to oneself, penetration into the Earth of *Hurqalya* and meeting with the celestial *alter ego*, these are the complementary aspects of the same event that proclaims the transmutation of the soul, its birth into the intermediary world.[17]

(vi) The Earth is then a *vision*, and geography a visionary geography. Hence it is the Image of itself and its own Image that the soul rediscovers and meets. This Image projected by it is at the same time the one which enlightens it and the one which reflects back to it, of which reciprocally it is itself the Image [...]

[...] this Energy or sacral light [Intelligence] is the power that causes springs to gush forth, the plants to germinate, the clouds to sail by, human beings to be born, [...] it is the power that lights up their intelligence.[18]

(vii) Ultimately what we call *physis* and physical is but the reflection of the world of the soul; there is no pure physics,

but always the physics of some definite psychic activity. So, to become aware of it is to see the world of the soul. [...] Then this reality that ordinary consciousness confers on physical things and events, as if they were autonomous realities, proves in fact to be the visionary reality of the soul. [...] The mystical Earth [...] represents the phenomenon of the Earth in its *absolute* state, that is, *absolved* from the empirical appearances displayed to the senses, and on the other hand, the *real* apparition restored by the transcendental Imagination alone. [...]

The way of seeing the Earth and the way of seeing the soul are the very same thing, the vision in which the soul perceives itself; this can be its *paradise,* and it can be its *hell.* When the mystic contemplates this universe it is himself (*nafs, Anima*), that he is contemplating.[19]

(Henry Corbin)

(viii) All that appears to us as a dimension of objects is not, in fact, really something concrete at all, but is an aspect of our own primordial state appearing to us.[20]

(Namkhai Norbu)

What we find referred to in all these passages about the mystic's experience of the natural environment is obviously connected with meditation, and the mystical experience sometimes called—perhaps misleadingly—absorption in the ocean of oneness, the "oceanic feeling."[21] But the writers here express this absorption not in terms of annihilation of all attributes in a sea of unity, but in terms of a conversation or meeting, with oneself, on a higher level than that normally suggested by the word *self-consciousness.* And it is as if the world of nature, of landscape, in all these passages is functioning as a mirror: and this is odd, for the Western mind is attuned to thinking that a mirror can reflect only the face placed in front of it. The sensation consistently invoked by the quoted remarks is of seeing a reflection of oneself in the very elements of the world which Rationalist or Cartesian consciousness insisted were not those of the self (or were indeed those of the not-self). The edifice of Western analytical philosophy (an edifice which many philosophers, such as Huston Smith, think is in an appalling state of dilapidation)[22] stems from that very notion which divides self from world. But here, in what look like paradoxical statements, it happens that in a certain state of consciousness (see chapters 2 and 4) an encounter may take place which is a recognition of reciprocal relation between two things hitherto thought separate. Because this recognition depends on the meditative process or the mystical state to come about, it may be that this state itself is no other than the soul[23] in its enabling aspect, allowing us to recognize, while the state lasts, that we *are expressed by* what we see as much as that we see anything. The fact that we do not normally realize our real condition causes us to feel separate and estranged from the world, which we then call "outer." The more it is felt to be outer, the more it becomes devalued, till the point comes where existentialists call the world *boue* (mud) because it is not self.

What we find described in the quoted passages—and what is recognized as the motivating experience of countless poems of the Romantic period—is the theophanic state,[25] in which seer, seeing, and seen are indistinguishable. This may not ultimately be other than what is called the oceanic feeling, but it is characterized in a way which gives a helpfully different insight into the degree and nature of this experience as it happens to or in a person, and how the elements of this world are involved in the experience the Romantic poets speak of, Shelley notably in "Mont Blanc" and the "Ode to the West Wind." This experience, says Henry Corbin, paraphrasing Ibn 'Arabi, "is not the place of mystical annihilations, of the abysses of negative theology, but the place of divine epiphanies, which do not volatilize the soul nor tear it away from the vision of itself, but on the contrary help it to be at last with itself and in itself."[26] Bachelard: "The dreamer's *cogito* moves off and goes to lend its being to things, to noises and to fragrances.... The book has just spoken to us of ourselves."[27]

Thus we find Coleridge, early in his career, with his conscious intentions placed in "fighting the bloodless fight/of science, freedom, and the Truth in Christ," "active and firm," nevertheless falling into a "tranquil muse upon tranquility" as a result of gazing at the landscape, and asking this:

> O! The one life within us and abroad
> Which meets all motion and becomes its soul,
> A light in sound, a sound-like power in light
>   [...] the mute still air
> Is Music slumbering upon her instrument.
>   [...]
> And what if all the animated nature
> Be but organic harps diversely fram'd,
> That tremble into thought, as o'er them sweeps
> Plastic and vast, one intellectual breeze
> At once the Soul of each, and God of all?[28]

It is clear from other parts of this poem that this apprehension of the outer *and* inner worlds, arising from a conversation between the "intellectual breeze" and the strings designed to respond to it—the divine and the human—takes place only in a state where

"rests the tir'd mind, and waking loves to dream."

Or where

Full many a thought uncall'd and undetained
And many idle flitting phantasies
Traverse my indolent and passive brain.[29]

This is one of the states of meditation, or a state closely approaching it, characterized by all the mystical traditions as being an abeyance of conscious direction, neither "calling" nor "detaining" images or thoughts, and putting the ratiocinating activity into sedation while opening up other less-used capacities of the psyche. Letting one's psyche, as it were, be "played," as Coleridge's harp is, by the "plastic and vast... intellectual breeze." This breeze is metaphysical Intellect, not a localized individual intellect; it is intellect as understood by the Persian, Jewish, and Islamic mystics, which Blake and Coleridge in later life came to describe as one of the sources of Imagination. Coleridge describes the same meditative state as:

Silent with swimming sense, yea, gazing round
On the wide landscape, gaze till all doth seem
Less gross than bodily; and of such hues
As veil the Almighty Spirit, when yet he makes
Spirits perceive his presence.[30]

Again in the last two lines the theophanic action is shown. It is an action that comes about only in this meeting, denoted in "makes/Spirits *perceive*." With a leaning ever further away from the Cartesian direction of observer to observed, Coleridge describes how sometimes

[...] the prospect through the gazing eye pours all its healthful greenness on the soul,[31]

a reversal of perspective that helps us to see the reciprocity which absolutely requires that a perception be at the same time a meeting, not of the living with dead matter, but of the living with the living, and more, of the living recognizing itself in the living. Bachelard puts it with characteristic acumen: "The world presents itself alternately as spectacle and as gaze."[32] In Coleridge's "Dejection Ode":

> … We receive but what we give
> And in our life alone does Nature live.
> … Would we aught behold of higher worth,
> Than that inanimate cold world allowed
> To the poor loveless ever-anxious crowd,
>   Ah! From the soul itself must issue forth
> A light, a glory, a fair luminous cloud
>   Enveloping the Earth,
> And from the soul itself must there be sent
>   A sweet and potent voice, of its own birth
> Of all sweet sounds the life and element![33]

In "Frost At Midnight," it is precisely the same state of meditation into which the speaker falls, which attracts a perception and description of the "divine conversation" once again, this time (as so often for Coleridge) on behalf of his child.

> … thou, my babe, shalt wander like a breeze
> By lakes and sandy shores, beneath the crags
> of ancient mountains, and beneath the clouds
> Which image in their bulk both lakes and shores,
> And mountain crags: so thou shalt see and hear
> The lovely shapes and sounds intelligible
> Of that eternal language, which thy God
> Utters, who from Eternity doth teach
> Himself in all, and all things in himself.
> Great Universal teacher! He shall mould thy
> spirit, and *by giving make it ask.*[34]

This Divinity, note that it is "thy God," is not the patriarchal punisher of a certain tradition of Judaeo-Christian religious order, but one the meeting with whom is prepared, experienced, here and now in relation to the so-called outer world which—who—is actually no other than the rapt gazer's revealed inner world. "The world reveals itself alternately as spectacle and as gaze" says Bachelard. "Everything which sparkles, sees."[35] Likewise for the Zoroastrian contemplative,

> terrestrial phenomena are more than phenomena: they are the hierophanies [...] which in beings and things, reveal *who* these beings and their things are, that is, who their heavenly person, the source of their *Xvarnah*, is.[36]

The Andalusian mystic Ibn 'Arabi writes, *a propos* of the unknowability of God as beyond the knowables,

> God has especially created one universe in our image (a universe corresponding to each one of us). When the mystic contemplates that universe it is himself, his own soul, that he contemplates in it.[37]

We may here understand by "the mystic" anyone in the state corresponding to that of a mystic, precisely that of Coleridge's speaker, "silent with swimming sense," "gazing till all both seem/Less gross than bodily."[38] This is the state which the esotericists say is the traversable "stairway" between the many levels[39] of one's self, which are obscured by the quotidian level (which is called by the mystics of Islam the *nasut*). The term "active imagination," used by Coleridge, Blake and Wordsworth, Jung and Corbin, must then be understood as active only in that it enables other levels of self-awareness to be reached, and not in the sense of busily or toilingly active. Coleridge contrasts the two actions, one meditative, the other ratiocinative, in his reflections on "having left a place of Retirement":

> oft when after honourable toil
> Rests the tir'd mind, and waking loves to dream.[40]

The Active Imagination is only engaged by releasing the mental tensions of what we are accustomed to calling intellectual work. This release is what the Buddhist practice likewise favors, and is related to the abandonment of concern with the supposed aims and fruits of work, matters which so often preoccupy the so-called busy or industrious mentality. It is interesting that in all Coleridge's poems that relate to this matter it is the turning from the mind in toil to the mind in abeyance (while contemplating elements of landscape) that makes possible an articulation of that kernel, the meeting with oneself in contemplation, which seems of such permanent interest to Coleridge and as having such mysterious power for the writers—one a critic, one a novelist, one a Romantic poet, one an esoteric scholar, one a Tibetan teacher—quoted at the beginning of this chapter.

It is not as if we were dealing with a matter that is totally other than the "beautiful sights" with which banal Romanticism obscures true Romanticism's origins; but rather much more besides: a journey into the interior of what makes it beautiful in the first place. And the converse, or dialogue, thus reached "by giving, mak[ing] it ask," can come about only when the customary tools of what passes for conversation in most instances are laid aside, abandoned, in the manner declared essential by the *Bhagavad Gita*, the Buddhist scriptures, the Sufi texts, and the Romantic poems alike.

What is at stake is the instancing of, and reflections upon, the essential spiritual hermeneutics[41] by which poetic states provoke in the writers of poems, and in readers, the situation that originates those states. It is this closing of the circle which makes the experience that the mystics in East and West term an intimate dialogue between living being and its descended, but rememorized, self. Art, too, said Okakura, "is of value only to the extent that it speaks to us. It might be a universal language if we ourselves were universal in our sympathies." The contrast between this possible state of being and that presupposed by our profane age as the opposition of the human machine and the inert medium of outer world, could hardly be greater.

From another aspect that contrast is reflected quite as precisely in ecology. In their absolute interdependence, the organic and other elements express the singular existence of the planet, but they are cast by abusers of the environment in the role of unrelated pieces, with the disastrous consequences that such an illusive perspective cannot but imply.[43] The divine conversation implied by the poets seeking the conditions of meditation is a restatement of the ecology of mind, homologous in every degree to the organic ecology but, in the age the Romantics lived in, as in ours, still unaccepted by the mentality which (with more than a touch of unintentional irony) claimed its descent from the "Enlightenment." But other voices are making themselves heard. Anthony Blake, a modern mystic, says

> There is the landscape of the earth: sea, rivers, mountains, trees, each with its special feeling. It is not a subjective projection, the feeling of the Romantic; it is perception of eternity through space. And this is what we enter into when we use a symbol or spatial arrangement to enlarge our vision.[44]

As we have seen, the essence of a theophanic vision of cosmos is that it offers a presentiment of Perfect Nature—in which knowledge of self, knowledge of God and knowledge of the outer world come about as, and are known to be, one and the same. The *horizons* of this landscape—"the perception of eternity through space"—speak through harmonic sympathy of the horizons of soul, which in turn are defined by the mystical knowledge of contingent being in relation to necessary being; and this relation is the essence, visually and spiritually, of a sense of *perspective*.

4

ACTIVE IMAGINATION & CREATIVE INTERMEDIARIES

Judge then of thy Own Self: thy eternal lineaments explore,
What is Eternal and what Changeable, and what annihilable.
The Imagination is not a state: it is the Human Existence
itself.

—BLAKE

"WHAT IS THE RIGHT, the virtuous feeling and consequent action," asked Coleridge, "when a man having long meditated upon and perceived a certain truth, finds another, a foreign writer, who has handled the same with an approximation to the truth as he had previously conceived it? Joy! Let truth make her voice audible!"[1] In answering his own question, Coleridge gives his blessing to anyone who, reflecting on the wide variety of speculations surrounding his theories of imagination and fancy, finds other instances of the same theory. It would be fair to say that the majority of literary critical accounts of Coleridge finish up by declaring that his thoughts or writings, at least on this subject, are inconsistent and confused. The critics usually adduce Coleridge's self-admitted failure to live up to his promises to write "a great work" on the imagination as evidence of the possibility that it was an unfinishable project, since untenable from the start.

More on the subject of his "failure" will be taken up later; for the moment let us remain with his suggestion that if we find a "foreign writer" whose matter corresponds to our own perceptions, the fact should be celebrated. "Joy! Let truth make her voice audible!" One contemplates with less joy the alternative reactions. Perhaps a grudging assent, tinged with regret on finding one's own formulation is not "original" (a symptom perhaps of Harold Bloom's celebrated "anxiety of influence")?[2] Perhaps an insistence that just because of differences in tonality or terminology, it cannot be the same truth at all? For Coleridge it seems neither possibility was as initially attractive as simply celebrating a coincidence. And, regarding the much misunderstood matter of the creative imagination in Coleridge and his contemporaries, there is many a coincidence to celebrate. One may be anticipated: that Ibn 'Arabi, the mystic whose metaphysics parallel Coleridge's by just such surprising coincidences as we've mentioned here, himself writes:

> If that which the prophets have brought agrees with what the thought-messengers have brought to their minds, so be it—and let them thank God for the agreement.[3]

Anyone who has travelled from European and English literature to the farther lands of Buddhist, Taoist, and Sufi metaphysics will discover not only one but many "foreign writers" whose ways of speaking about the imagination and creativity are handled not only with the same approximation to the truth as Coleridge conceived it, but with a coherence and detail that appear to be moving toward a level which Coleridge himself constantly felt he was just failing to reach. It is as though there exists, in Coleridge's version of the metaphysics of imagination, a sketch or landmark indicator of the territory that was not only within the experience of some of the mystics of the Near East and further afield but quite demonstrably within their power to express in terms actually more thorough than Coleridge's proved to be, or which at least, to turn the matter round, confirm Coleridge's thought to be less haphazard that it has appeared to commentators without knowledge of the esoteric material. It is certainly true that the writer of this work, having fairly "long meditated on" Coleridge's ideas on imagination and heard many contemporaries and commentators dismiss them as "idealism," "rambling metaphysics," "notoriously elusive and probably confused," "logocentric," "phallocentric," experienced a considerable surprise—not to say joy—on discovering that many seminal texts in the esoteric tradition amount to at once a fuller discussion of the matter, and a confirmation that Coleridge's valuation of the imagination was not the only one of its kind. Certainly, looked at in the light of the oriental metaphysical examinations of the same topic, his account of it was far from confused.

The academic's question must arise and may I hope be quickly answered: if Coleridge's ideas do agree with those of the gnostics, Sufis, and Vedantists, are we to suppose he had access to these texts (which, in the case of some, it appears almost certain he did not)? Or did he have texts from a tradition so intimately homologous to those of the Sufis and Vedantists that he formulated the same content "by proxy," as it were? Neither avenue of reply is very satisfactory, but the second is more helpful than the first. And even the second only answers to the evidential aspect of the situation, which is that there is a direct route from Coleridge back to the Middle and Far East via the German Romantic philosophers, Böhme, and the European Cabala.[4]

The answer I propose is the answer Jung and the esotericists would probably also give, namely, that there can be no talk either of conscious influence or of proof by verifying Coleridge's reading lists that is not of a fairly superficial type (though one of his reading lists did include Iamblichus, Proclus, Ficino, Thomas Taylor "the English pagan," and "Theuth the Egyptian"). "The trap of historical thinking, which assumes no basic interior source for knowledge and has to seek literary and superficial inspiration, is constantly avoided by the Sufi."[5] Idries Shah reminds us that what the esoteric mystics enunciate is the singular ground alike of consciousness, of reason, and of the world (the world, that is, seen as outer). So the principle according to which any formulations arose, Coleridge's included, is "the anthropic principle,"[6] that is, the esoteric principle, and according to that order, it can necessarily be no other than the principle he is seen to have expressed in his metaphysical speculations. (On the evidence of his poetic work, it would appear also that Coleridge had personal experience of the action of this principle, not only the ability to formulate it in speculative work.) The old image of the waves and the sea occurred again to Kathleen Raine, who wrote that Coleridge's projected "greater work" in fact

> did exist; it was never embodied in writing, but, as a mental entity, it was there, throwing up, ocean-like, now one wave-crest, now another, each bearing witness to a vast underlying unity. Coleridge's writings are fragmentary, but his thought is coherent, consistent, and whole: so that from the smallest indications—a mere paragraph—we are able to see how any particular conclusion is logically related to the complete system. *Such consistency is the mark of truly creative thinking.*[7]

Jungian thought, and the esoteric and experiential principle of Tao, Vedanta, Buddhism, and Sufism would, in making this point about creative thinking, go even further. It is, strictly speaking, not Coleridge's thought that is coherent, consistent, and whole, but thought itself that is so. Jung's writings have come in for very similar criticisms—voluminousness, fragmentariness—as have Coleridge's, but much the same as Raine says of Coleridge could be said in Jung's favor, too, that in his work, "a mental entity ... was there, [...] throwing up now one wave-crest, now another—each logically related to the complete system." It will probably not have escaped the student of the new sciences that this situation, in which each fragment is logically related to the whole, has an analogy in the hologram which, when split, splintered, or shattered, reproduces in the fragment the image carried by the original whole. This analogy is helpful when it comes to studying the often perplexing verbal formulations of such as Plato, Plotinus, Ibn 'Arabi, Paracelsus, Jakob Böhme, Blake, and Coleridge, formulations which mention by name (and often very varied names) the splinters and the process by which that splintering happens.

What then, can the confluence or coincidence of the mystical texts and Coleridge's system be celebrated for? First there is a suggestion made all the plainer by each accumulating coincidence: that the criticisms made against Coleridge's system (which, interestingly, are criticisms also made by most philosophers when they oppose mysticism)[8] are based on the assumption that language is the basic unit of awareness and that *just because it can express philosophical systems it also exhaustively does so.* That is an assumption of priority[9] which Coleridge openly contested in his work as an essayist and tacitly moved beyond in his visionary excursions and poetic work.

The case can be simplified as follows. The philosopher believes discursive understanding is the basic unit of philosophy, and dismisses as unphilosophic any formulations of language which are in the *genre*, but which nevertheless do not take discursive understanding as the basic unit, but take it only as one mode among others. It is precisely in order to oppose or question this dismissal, which cuts off the fuel supply of the philosophical undertaking, that Coleridge formulated his theory of imagination and fancy. That is why although it is quite useful it is not really enough, nor to the point, to say in Coleridge's defence that he refutes the empirical philosophers using their own terms on their own ground. It may be that he

---

71

does so, but to prove it is only to remain at the level these philosophers wish us and themselves to occupy. "Westerners want proof, more proof and still more proof, and all the time they try to prove that the proof is wrong."[10] Coleridge's intention was to move up from there, to "shift the center of the human mind from the discursive understanding to a faculty beyond normal consciousness, akin to vision."[11]

The aim, then? To identify the discursive linguistic unit as inadequate, and next, to move to a level on the return from which ordinary consciousness may again use words to point to where it has come from "in its flights."[12] Sometimes perhaps the Romantic poets, Blake and Shelley more than Coleridge, it must be admitted, wrote parts of their work during such flight; and around the expansion of possibilities which "poetic diction,"[13] "the wings of poesy"[14] affords language, a great deal of Romantic theory has been, and usefully, centered. But alongside appreciating all composition achieved "in flight," it could never be forgotten that to produce—and cause to be read—a poem depended in the end on a pact with the discursive machinery of grammar, parts of speech, and the subject-object relation. About this pact more is found in chapters 2 and 8, but what matters here is that for writing down, printing, publication, and reading, the pact was necessary, and the re-evocation of the state of vision beyond discursive understanding, a chancy affair to say the least, depended very much on the state of receptivity of the reader, and even more on whether the reader assumed that the limits of language were the same as the limits of being or of awareness. Hence the great emphasis laid by Coleridge, and Heidegger, Jung, and Fromm after him, on the distinction in some degrees of consciousness between knowing and being, and the identity of these two at another, highly elevated, degree. The energy required to move through these degrees was recognized as being the energy of active imagination.

The coincidence to celebrate is that poets and mystics alike appear to have wanted to make this fact known. This shifting of the center of the human awareness from one degree to another is the central matter, no less for Coleridge and the other Romantic poets discussed in this book whose work endorses his research than for the metaphysic and process of esoteric education according to the Taoist, Buddhist, or Sufi. The common insistence that these Romantic and mystical modes of awareness are superstitious, deranging, irrational, untenable, and so on, is made nearly always from a quarter which estimates that reality is only in the degree of the relative and discursive. This is the only point of view from which criticism of the Romantic and esoteric work can have meaning, and once this fact is recognized, that meaning is quite as limited as the degree to which it corresponds.

And it is precisely being stuck in this degree which the total composition of the human psyche cannot ultimately tolerate because it is not "the natural place for man."[15] That is why the images of flight and excavation, heights, and depths, have been and remain such powerful impulses in the arts and in psychology,[16] where the artist, dreamer, is *in flight,* and the therapist or healer trained in one or other of the traditions of *depth* psychology. It is the overwhelming agreement amongst the saints, psychologists, artists, and healers of the twentieth century that to neglect areas of the human totality other than the rationalizing, ego-bound, everyday area is the cause in the psyche of what manifest metabolically as malnutrition and starvation. Gurdjieff used to say that man's sustenance comes from "air, food, and impressions," and behind him was an "ocean" of thought of which his expositions in psychology and esoteric science were, in Raine's phrase, simply one "wave-crest." To mention the others for the evidence-hungry can, alas, take no more interesting a form than a long list of names and books.

It is obviously the "impressions" aspect of human sustenance that artists, psychologist, and aestheticians are mostly concerned with, and which concerns anyone who asks the question why imagination should be of such consuming importance to Coleridge. To remind the thinking reader or reading thinker that there was such a power was, equally, to constate the opportunity open to everyone to move into those degrees of awareness which would afford a sustenance composed of impressions from yet other levels, all of them related to the human's reason for existence.[17]

An attitude that sets itself against Coleridge's ideas on imagination commonly takes the form of asking why it should be as important for us to explore Imagination as it was for Coleridge, with the implication that his interest was personal, a side issue, or an arcane backwater of enquiry. What follows is an attempt to reply.

Henry Corbin, the scholar of Islamic and Persian esotericism, draws attention to G. T. Fechner's anecdote: on a spring morning Fechner suddenly found that "the earth is an angel, such a gorgeously real angel, so like a flower." But, he adds with melancholy, "nowadays an experience like this is dismissed as *imaginary*. It is taken for granted that the earth is a spherical body; as for getting to know more about what it is, this is just a matter of research in mineralogical collections."[18] That anecdote is the prelude to Corbin's study of the Zoroastrian and Sufi perspective of a metaphysical terrain or "celestial earth." What Fechner's remark points to is just as relevant to European Romanticism as it is to the object of Corbin's exploration. The principle, experience, and conflicting valuations of Fechner's imaginative expression are together the real subject of Corbin's book and of any serious study of the Romantics' interest in nature. Their focus, in short, can be substituted without loss for any imaginative corpus, as it was by Corbin, who applied the same ideas to four sub-traditions in turn.[19] He continues:

It is quite obvious that the mental vision of the Angel of the Earth [...] is not a sensory experience. If, by logical habit, we classify this fact as imaginary, the question nonetheless remains as to what can justify an identification of what is imaginary with what is arbitrary and unreal, the question as to whether representations deriving from physical perception are the only ones to be considered as *real* knowledge, whether physically verifiable events alone can be evaluated as facts. We must ask ourselves whether the invisible action of forces that have their purely physical expression in natural processes may not bring into play psychic energies that have been neglected or paralyzed by our habits, and directly touch an Imagination which, far from being arbitrary invention, corresponds to that Imagination which the alchemists called *Imaginatio vera* and which is the (Paracelsian) *astrum in homine.*[20]

We can already begin to see how closely Corbin's expansion of the realm of the knowable relates to Coleridge's and the Romantics' view, even down to singling out the paralysis of habit, what Shelley called the "film of familiarity that obscures," and Coleridge called "the lethargy of custom." Corbin's description also extends to the action of this imagination so familiar to us from Coleridge:

The active imagination thus induced will not produce some arbitrary, even lyrical, construction standing between us and "reality," but will, on the contrary, function directly as a faculty and organ of knowledge just as *real* as—if not more real than—the sense organs. However, it will perceive in the manner proper to it: the organ is not a sensory faculty but an *archetype image* that it possessed from the beginning: it is not something derived from any outer perception. And the property of this image will be precisely that of effecting the transmutation of sensory data, their resolution into the purity of the subtle world, in order to restore them as symbols to be deciphered, the "key" being imprinted in the soul itself. Such perception through the Imagination is therefore equivalent to a "dematerialization": it changes the datum impressed upon the senses in a pure mirror, a spiritual transparency; thus it is that the Earth and the things and beings of the Earth, raised to incandescence, allow the apparition of their Angels to penetrate to the visionary intuition. This being so, the authenticity of the event and its full reality consist essentially of this visionary act and of the apparition vouchsafed by it. Thus is constituted this intermediary world, a world of archetypal celestial figures which the active Imagination alone is able to comprehend. This Imagination does not construct something unreal, but *unveils* the hidden reality. Its action, in short, is [...] that of alchemical meditation: to occultate the apparent, to manifest the hidden. It is in this intermediary world that those known as the *urafa*, the mystical gnostics, have meditated tirelessly, *gnosis* here being taken to mean that perception which grasps the object not in its objectivity, but as a sign, an intimation, and announcement that is finally the soul's annunciation to itself.[21]

Here in full outline is what Coleridge called Imagination in his celebrated, but scattered, comments in his letters and *Biographia Literaria*. But here the description is centered as fully as it can be on its subject. *Imagination* is as much a reality as physically verifiable data; it is effective in the lives of people because it is *active*, and its world, the *intermediary*, is the "place" that it is active in. The people it is especially active in are gnostic mystics, anyone given to the type of contemplation or meditation referred to, among whom it would be impossible not to include the entranced Blake, Coleridge, Shelley, and Wordsworth. "You perhaps smile at *my* calling another poet a *mystic*; but verily I am in the very mire of common place compared to Mr. Blake, ana- or rather apo-calyptic poet and painter!" wrote Coleridge in 1818.[22]

Coleridge's work on the Imagination was neither the studied repetition of a tradition nor the solitary devisings of a maverick. A condensed account of his fortunes where this work is concerned may help to show the coherence of thought and intention that his critics have so constantly denied him, as well as serve to illustrate his living connection with the impulse and perspective of the esoteric gnostics. By his own account, "after [he] had successively studied in the schools of Locke, Berkeley, Leibniz, and Hartley, [he] could find in neither of them an abiding place for [his] reason," and he "was for a while disposed to admit that the sole practicable employment for the human mind was to observe, to collect, and to classify." That was the first stage in his search, which brought him to the situation of rationalism, still today the limiting regulation according to which most philosophers and academics pursue their work (and dismiss other regulations as speculative). This stage also afforded him his first definition of fancy as opposed to Imagination, the "discursive understanding which forms for itself general notions and terms of classification for the purpose of comparing or arranging phenomena."[23] But he "soon felt, that human nature itself fought up against this wilful resignation of intellect, and as soon did [he] find, that the scheme taken with all its consequences and cleared of all inconsistencies was not less impracticable than contra-natural."[24]

There are several things to mark in this summing up of Coleridge's journey so far. First, that he found his own "reason" could find no "abiding place" in the rationalist position, any more than it could in the strictly Idealist. That suggests his sense of the word *reason* was not the one understood in the phrase the "age of reason" (eighteenth century Enlightenment): if it had been, his own reason would presumably have found a home there. Second, that in accepting rationalism as the "sole practicable occupation for the human mind," he still perceived a "resignation of intellect" which made such acceptance not good enough. So we find in Coleridge's reluctant Rationalism a still homeless *reason* and a resigned *intellect*. This apparent paradox suggests that hidden meanings for *reason* and *intellect* presented themselves, meanings which neither rationalists nor idealists had taken into account. Third, given these things, Coleridge found a full application of them not only impracticable in the end, but "contra-natural," against nature.

So far so good, or perhaps not so good. Those were the facts, but there are implications, too. What is certainly implied here is that for Coleridge, reason and intellect were neither defined nor exhausted by the function of "observing, collecting and classifying," and also at the same time they *were* related, somehow, to nature. The problems raised here can be appreciated in view of the "general belief" that rationalism had the best explanation of the human condition.

Coleridge's search went on, compelled by these very real problems. His involvement with Wordsworth, and his other activities in poetic writing, obviously supplied some address to matters not "contra-natural," matters concerning that to which his intellect was not so much "wilfully resigned" as engrossed. He began to feel, as did all the Romantics in various different ways, that devising, and ingenuity, and wit, the mainstays of the eighteenth century poetic tradition, left many aspects of the human mind without an "abiding place," and evinced the feeling that, taken to extremes, as the eighteenth century philosophy invited it to be, it would have a "contra-natural" effect.

He went on. "Repeated meditations led me first to suspect, and a more intimate analysis of the human facilities, their appropriate marks, functions and effects, matured my conjecture into full conviction, that fancy and imagination were two distinct and widely different faculties, instead of being, according to the general belief, either two names with one meaning or, at furthest, the lower and higher degree of one of the same power... that two conceptions perfectly distinct are confused under one of the same word." Out of these meditations we could say that Coleridge distilled a resolve which was at once to present his contemporaries with some much needed news and to revive a perspective which was older than writing itself. "Now were it once fully ascertained, that this division were [...] grounded in nature [...], the theory of the fine arts, and of poetry in particular, could not [...] but derive some additional and important light."[25] So we see a resolve, formulated first in terms of the intellectual life, "furnishing a torch of guidance," so Coleridge hoped, "to the philosophical critic, and ultimately to the poet himself."[26] And he, as a poet of psychic states, well knew that the further one moved from the so-called "intellectual" to the "creative" field, the more "intimate," living, and "grounded in nature" one's being would become. We have seen that in his early searches he already guessed that the "general belief" of his contemporaries about reason and intellect left something of his own reason and intellect unaddressed; now perhaps a step forward could be made in his discovery of a way of talking about imagination that would prevent its real meaning being "confounded with the usual import of the word."[27] In a sense, a marriage, a *conjunctio mystica*, of the philosophic and creative forces, formerly thought as divided, could come about. To have articulated this "marriage" was Coleridge's peculiar grace afforded by time, place, and circumstance: the meaning of life might be more deeply comprehended through the living of it in its most direct facing, a facing we have described in chapter 3 as conversation or meeting.

Meditations were no doubt "repeated" and further extended, but the outcome, in Coleridge's most famous enunciation, is a description of extraordinary clarity, firmness, and brevity, which characterizes at once the nature of imagination, the nature of fancy, and the intermediate zone. According to this description there is (i) Primary Imagination, (ii) Secondary Imagination, and (iii) Fancy. It will not take long to quote it in full:

(i) The imagination then I consider as primary or secondary. The primary Imagination I hold to be the living power and prime agent of all human perception, and as a repetition in the finite mind of the eternal act of creation in the infinite I AM.

(ii) The secondary I consider as an echo of the former, co-existing with the conscious will, yet still as identical with the primary in the kind of its agency, and differing only in degree, and in the mode of its operation. It dissolves, diffuses, dissipates, in order to re-create; or where this process is rendered impossible, yet still, at all events it struggles to idealize and to unify. It is essentially vital, even as all objects (as objects) are essentially fixed and dead.

(iii) Fancy, on the contrary, has no other counters to play with but fixities and definites. The Fancy is indeed no other than a mode of memory, emancipated from the order of time and space; and blended with, and modified by, that empirical phenomenon of the will, which we express by the word choice. But equally with the ordinary memory, it must receive all its materials ready-made from the law of association.[28]

This description has been the subject of such enormous critical debate, debate which most often ends with (at worst) dismissal, or (at best) charges of confusion and obscurity, that I am tempted to render it diagrammatically to show that it is more straightforward than might be supposed.

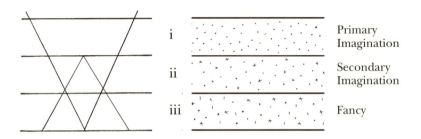

i		Primary Imagination
ii		Secondary Imagination
iii		Fancy

The diagram, just like Coleridge's verbal account, can have meaning only if the three zones are taken to be only distinguished, rather than divided, from one another. This appreciation of what is from one point of view distinct but not separated is one of the metaphysical principles and intellectual foundations of mystical gnosis. (Another "diagrammatic" analogy is to speak not of distinctions or divisions but of zones englobed by zones, like Russian dolls, or Chinese boxes. Coleridge's text initiates this form, in that qualities of the second zone are present in the paragraph on the first zone, namely, "the finite mind"; and qualities of the third zone are present in the paragraph on the second, namely "conscious will" and "fixed.") To appreciate that in certain states the human being participates in all three levels, even though each level has a description of its own state, is to dispel the so-called confusion of Coleridge's thought and to do away simultaneously with the nagging doubt as to the intellectual validity of the Romantics' special interest in the dream/trance/gnostic states and their relationship to human consciousness.[29] This interest is paralleled in modern poetics, for instance Allen Ginsberg's use of Tibetan esotericism and Vedantic metaphysics. The diagram could be re-drawn in global form, the only drawback being that fancy, seeming central in the diagram, is actually central only in that it pertains to "this world" rather than the next, the invisible and metaphysical worlds.

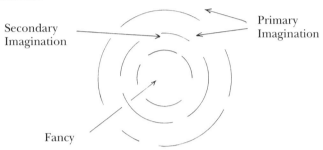

Does it require a book as involved and complex as Barfield's *What Coleridge Thought* to come to terms with this matter, which Coleridge himself could express with as terse a wording as "Genius must have talent as its complement and implement, just as in like manner Imagination must have fancy. In short, the higher intellectual powers can only act through a corresponding energy of the lower."?[30] I do not know. But what we are being asked to contemplate we already contemplate in the biosphere. Coleridge's treatment of imagination is nothing other than an ecology of consciousness.

This ecology, the imaginative eco-system, is identical in character to what was known by the Sufis and Iranian theosophists. We can begin to get a taste of it even before arriving at examples of their expositions. Coleridge did not stop at his characterization of the relation between the modes of imagination and fancy. He went further and found a new, undreamed of, literally unlimited range in the very *reason* to which, at the beginning of his metaphysical search, rationalist philosophy gave so few "abiding places." And in discovering that the abiding place of reason was none other than the canopy of the heavens, the roof of the world, Coleridge was in the company of the gnostics themselves:

> The reason, (not the abstract reason, not the reason as the mere organ of science, or as the faculty of scientific principles and schemes a priori; but reason) as the integral spirit of the regenerated man, reason substantiated and vital, *"one only, yet manifold,* one seeing all, and going through all understanding; the *breath* of the power of God, and a pure influence from the *glory* of the Almighty; which *remaining in itself* regenerateth all other powers, and in all ages entering into holy souls, mak[ing] them *friends of God* and prophets" (Wisdom of Solomon, 100, vii); this reason without being either the sense, the understanding [fancy], or the imagination, contains all three within itself, even as the mind contains its thoughts and is present in and through them all; or as the expression pervades the different features of an intelligent countenance.[31]

Quoting so freely from the *Apocrypha* to crown his metaphysical system, Coleridge invites us to examine that quoted chapter; and opening it we discover that what he quotes as being a fitting description of this elevated Reason is actually a description of Wisdom and the creative feminine. The *Apocrypha* actually reads: "For she is the breath of the power of God," whereas Coleridge substitutes the neutral gender later in his quotation. Whatever his reason for doing that, it is clear that the aptness of the prophetic quotation to his sense of metaphysical nature was, alike and equally, from a source which earned adepts of the esoteric tradition one of their epithets, the *fedele d'amore,* wayfarers of love.[32] One might hazard the guess that Coleridge changed the pronoun for fear of misunderstanding or repudiation from the orthodox Christians whose company he frequented. But Solomon's exaltation of reason the creator as

Feminine is in harmony with Rumi's: "She is not the being whom sensual desire takes as its object. She is creator, it should be said. She is not a creature."[33] In the Aramaic language the Holy Spirit is feminine. In the Gospel according to the Hebrews, Christ speaks of "my mother the Holy Spirit."[34] Whether or not we go further and speak of Jung's mother archetype in this context, we may still constate from all these examples that the "inner court" of the Judaeo-Christian tradition is by no means the masculine monolith which cultural theories in general are determined to account it.

We have now arrived at a point where we can return to and pick up Coleridge's wistful speculation about "a pilgrimage to the deserts of Arabia to find the man who could make me understand how the one can be many."[35] In the world into which we are about to enter (the world of symbols, symbolic and synchronic analogy, not that of empirical proof) we may say that one of the gnostics, whom Sophia the divine wisdom taught about the "one only yet manifold" Existence, lived indeed in the desert of Arabia, and his name and school, though lost to a lot of European history, nevertheless watered the roots of German Romanticism.

Could Coleridge have been making a sympathetic or theurgic appeal to the Sufis, the dwellers of the desert, some of whose masters, like Rumi, or Muhyiddin Ibn 'Arabi, spent all their lives speaking about and reconciling the one and the many, and invoking Love as the Reconciler in the affair? What we can readily find in the nature of exact parallels in Coleridgean and Sufi metaphysics suggests perhaps that Coleridge need not have made the pilgrimage, because the truth of the matter expressed itself in his own interior. And the parallels subsist not in metaphysics alone but in a taste for imagery which suggests Coleridge's preoccupation with the night sky is just that which invites a desert visionary, where there are so few buildings, clouds, and trees to obstruct his sight.

5

THE FOUR WORLDS

Now I a fourfold vision see
And a fourfold vision is given to me.

—BLAKE

The various worlds are, properly speaking, states, not
places, although it is possible to describe them symbolically
as such; the Sanskrit word *loka* which serves to designate
them, and which is identical to the Latin *locus*, contains
within itself the indication of this special symbolism.

—RENÉ GUÉNON

THE ROMANTICS' THEORY OF IMAGINATION involves a
proposition that goes against the grain of our habitual way of
seeing the world. The proposition is that humanity lives not in
one world only, but simultaneously in more than one world.
While the mystic may be expected to propose this, it might
come as a surprise that for a poet, also, imagination is the
means of traffic between worlds, a facilitator of transformative
movement. One of the reasons why Coleridge's theory of
imagination is often dismissed as speculation is that unfortu-
nately, according to Corbin, "the idea that imagination has a
noetic value, that it is an organ of knowledge because it 'creates' being, is not readily compatible with our habits."[1] For
cultural empiricists the worlds of active Imagination are only
entertaining illusions. But to the esoteric schools, for instance
the Neoplatonists and Sufis, they are facts, to be taken into
account at every moment and in every assessment of life. For
at any moment four worlds are potentially involved.

We must make ourselves aware at the outset that neither for the poets nor for the esoteric schools is the study of the other worlds undertaken to earn "rewards" or set up a safe-haven against the moment of death. Less as a religious consolation, more as a science, the study of the other worlds is undertaken in response to the question of questions, which concerns the sense and purpose of life on earth, and human life in particular. In this spirit Coleridge explored science, mathematics, philosophy as well as theology. Just as Wordsworth's does, his poetic work seeks to induce in practice the visionary state which in its exposition or explanatory function it describes. And by the time Wordsworth and Coleridge along with Shelley and Blake came to the "practice" of the poetic state, the categories of theology, politics, science could be temporarily abated, or melded; at any rate it was meaning that was sought, not simply such hard knowledge as may be connoted by the word *science*, not such comfort or relief as is nearly always connoted by the derogatory uses of *other worldly* and *other worlds*. So the sentimental associations of "other worlds" must be set aside; so equally must the thought that the self is transported from this world to the next, as if it were a parcel being posted; so, in turn, must the notion that a person progresses in fixed sequence from world to world in a kind of "career" in time.

What freed the Romantics from the delusions just mentioned and enabled them to bring about a rupture in the world-boundaries is that they had precise indications about the contemplative/imaginative state that made it clear that the terms of discussion of the everyday state, of this world, could not be applied to the further states. "The mood has to be delicately educated, so [as to] no longer impress its own restriction on all our experiences."[2] Like the work of Jung, the poets' work suggested psychologically what a scientist such as David Bohm[3] has since been able to put into the terms used by physics, mathematics, and biology, namely that the further dimensions cannot be approached using the tools of only this dimension of experience. Here is the meaning, then, of the recurrent imagery in Romanticism and mysticism of the passing away of self *and* of the perceptions "proper" to that self. Similarly, the extinction of time so often referred to amongst the works of the visionary poets suggests again the same move, from the world of conditions which our post-rationalist education has taught is the only world, into another world or worlds.

Now, in the kind of society or community where the existence of other worlds is taken to be neither fancy nor "entertaining notion" but fact, it may seem that the Romantic poets' emphasis on suggesting means of opening oneself to the action of the other worlds is either disproportionate or needless. Such a community might well have reason to turn to other matters less "mixed." But in the West, at this period in history, this type of community, even this type of school of thought is rare, and certainly the exception rather than the norm. And it is the function of a "school" such as Romanticism, or any other esoteric school, or indeed depth psychology, to address its particular station in historical time with facts that this time needs, or which it misses, or which it has fallen asleep to:

> Through knowledge of the laws that condition the physical world we are able to manipulate it. At the present time, man is very successful at doing this, but he fails to realize that this does nothing for his being and even takes him further away from contact with *life*. In spite of it, we still cling to this world and do not want to leave it.[4]

J. G. Bennett wrote this in the 1970s. More than a hundred years before, Shelley wrote of the same matter in almost identical terms:

87

Cultivation of those sciences which have enlarged the limits of the empire of man over the external world, has, for want of the poetical faculty, proportionally circumscribed those of the internal world; and man, having enslaved the elements, remains himself a slave.[5]

Blake, even more succinct, said,

Man has closed himself up, till he sees all things thro' narrow chinks in his cavern.[6]

It may be said with certainty, the further we explore the experience of the Romantics, that their particular predilection for imaginative/contemplative involvement was a response to a spiritual hunger evident in the condition of society then, which has, as is all too evident, not changed much in the one and a half centuries that divides Shelley's comment from Bennett's; or E. G. Howe's: "What we have gained in outsight we have lost in insight."[7]

So the poets' reclamation of imagination, of "the shaping spirit," just like the esoteric training offered by Taoist, Buddhist, and Sufi schools, is not a refuge in theology, it is an inner journey undertaken in the knowledge that the traveller is the instrument, not simply the container, of the knowledge and understanding with which he or she may come into touch. The poet or the mystic is not going to a repository of materials to build up a store of knowledge; under that model, journeyers still imagine themselves to be as they are before the journey started, and imagine that they can foresee a point in their "career" when the knowledge will have been collected. But that attitude fails to take account of the action of creativity, which acts, as Goethe observed, in such unaccountable ways upon a person as to change the entire mode, conditions, means, and perception of life. The forms with which the journey began do not always fit the further stages, let alone the end. Goethe likened the way of transformation to the stages through which a caterpillar becomes a butterfly; the changes being so radical as well as so abrupt that they are not anywhere near as "causally predictable" as that a stone, say, will roll down a slope and stop at the bottom. Coleridge's noting that the Greek word for soul, *psyche*, means butterfly[8] may not be insignificant, and Blake's depictions of the soul as butterfly are known from several engravings:[9] such an observation of the peculiar evidence offered by the metamorphosis of insects the English Romantics evidently shared with Goethe.[10]

The metamorphosis of the butterfly suggests how the creative action, Active Intelligence, *draws* the individuated being *through* stages, from "world" to "world," rather than perpetuating its existence at one stage only as though, so to speak, the caterpillar stage were permanent (or final).

There is an added profound felicity in Goethe's and Coleridge's comparison here that goes to the heart of the matter of esoteric initiation and of the poetic experience and practice. It is this. The case of the butterfly's and the human's possible metamorphosis is similar in that although the caterpillar does not stay stuck at the caterpillar stage but is drawn *through* two stages into its culminating form, still its culminating form has not left this life behind; on the contrary, its adult state is in fact its perfection: bright colour, graceful form, flight, ability to reproduce, and presence *in the physical world.* The enlightened human's state is similar.[11] Contrary to the popularized understanding of the mystical journey, this world is not left behind at all as the stages of initiation are passed through or accepted into one's being. "A man who has the freedom to live in the second world," according to Bennett, "does not on that account turn his back on the physical world. If he did this, he would be repeating, but in reverse, the mistakes from which he had just been liberated."[12] The mystical journey must be understood from both directions, that is, the journey from one's accident to one's origin, and then back to this world, in a transformed understanding of the determinations of the accident. "It is the freedom to live in the second world that enables us to live rightly in the first world."[13]

And here we come to another vital understanding of the deeper relation of the Romantics' and mystics' work to the reality of "this" world, a situation which political action attempts on its own with only limited success to concern itself with. Without the assistance of what it often outlaws as irrelevant nonsense, that is, without the assistance of creative impulses that poets and mystics are the agents of, political work cannot truly and therefore cannot effectively act with the compassion politics invokes. Again it was Shelley who saw this in its sharpest definition.

> To what but a cultivation of the mechanical arts in a degree disproportioned to the presence of the creative faculty, which is the basis of all knowledge, is to be attributed the abuse of all invention for abridging and combining labour, to the exasperation of the inequality of mankind? [...]

> The cultivation of poetry is never more to be desired than at periods when, from an excess of the selfish and calculating principle, the accumulation of [...] materials of external life exceed [...] the power of assimilating them to the internal laws of human nature.[14]

And it is the *internal laws of human nature* which, according to the esoteric community, ultimately request their actualization *in four worlds at once*, not only in the single world expressed in time, space, mechanism, cause, and effect. The question constantly needing to be asked and reasked is what this *human nature* is. Thus also for the poets, whose source is, as it is for the esotericists, creativity itself: whatever state it is that improves the human's receptivity is the one most willingly then and there to be sought. This is the inner meaning of their trances. Unlike the theorists of today, they knew that human problems tackled by the political order could never be alleviated only from the level of the political, but only at the same time from a world beyond. Compassion is the link between the mystical and political ways. Ignoring it has neither any meaning nor any future. But a false habit of division of fields causes them to be separated in thought. So the Romantics will always be misunderstood if they are seen, as they have been so often, to be either social activists with more or less credibility, or else visionaries abstracted from all social duty.

The creative principle is itself the action of compassion at a certain, admittedly high, level. This is common knowledge amongst the Sufi ways of transformation.[15] Once the level of human action and reaction is considered, the conditions obviously appear far more complex and various but any success is only to be credited to the relationship being at a level closer to the source of the kind indicated. For the other worlds to become open to any exploration at all, therefore, the current habits of thought, which belong to one world only, must be laid aside. The hierarchical aspect implicit in the last paragraph, for instance, which is liable to inflame the indignation of the socialist, changes (as completely as the caterpillar does when proceeding to the chrysalis) as soon as it is possible to go out of the habitual concept of self from which most objections to hierarchy derive. Despite an apparent cultural wall of "faith versus doubt" between them, the Buddhist and the deconstructionist come very close indeed to one another here in their statement that the self, the subject, the personality around which most expectations of life, knowledge, and achievement are based, in reality has no existence. This matter, giving new significance to the time-honored Romantic cliché "dead to the world" is actually the starting point for entering into the next world. For the sake of the world one wishes (perhaps politically) to help, the need is to die to it. Such is the Buddhist's view and it is not alone in suggesting that each "death" avails a birth into the next level. One name for the availer is creativity. Coleridge's creative life, like the lives of many true artists, faced the terror of the *death* and the joy of the *birth* referred to above. In working out his principles of creative imagination, he also simultaneously hit upon an indication of the four worlds.

It remains to attempt an account of the four worlds. Such accounts are very rare in European literary studies, and of great value in returning Coleridge's and Blake's remarks on the degrees of being to a recognizable tradition. The nearest that English literature came to an account of these worlds, and in technical rather than experiential terms, was the Renaissance conception of the ladder of being, but it was more often the butt of satirists' ridicule than it was a map of human experience and consciousness. The account given here is a conspectus of about fifteen different expressions which, if they are compared, will be seen to be alike in their central purport. Owing to the position of language with relation to the four worlds, the designation *worlds* is approximate only, and could be substituted by *presences, realms, kingdoms, degrees,* depending on the point of view adopted by the speaker. And it is important, as an exponent of this teaching has said:

> To make anything useful out of these descriptions of the higher worlds we need to be able to bring ourselves to see the limitations of our thought and understanding. [...] Once people have learned how to relate it to their own experience, it becomes possible for them to understand and talk about things which otherwise would be too elusive.[16]

The first world (or last, depending on the order the account happens to take) is, *so to speak*, the familiar world touched, seen, tasted, heard, weighed, measured, subject to the elementary laws of classical physics (see p. 53). Its presence in consciousness is the memory of outer impressions, and consecutive logic; it is also the world which space and time express. For the strictly empirical or atheistic criterion, this first world is the only reality whatsoever. For the mystical or esoteric criterion, the first world is the furthest extent, entification or solidification of Being. As in William Blake's phrase "The five senses are the chief inlets of soul in this age,"[17] the first world is the world admitted, in-let, through the five senses. It corresponds to the names given it by the main esoteric traditions, the *rupa, samsara, nasut, alam al Mulk, alemi ajsam*, corporeity, the physical world, the world of observation and evidence.[18] This world is also to a great extent the world which language appropriates and describes, but to this there are important exceptions which come up in another chapter. Nevertheless, the extent to which language is linked up with this first world is so great that language and "construction of world/consciousness" are held by linguistic philosophy to be synonymous.

The second world is much less easy to refer to in terms that are not misleading, but it is the world that most of the poets, and much of this book, are concerned with from various points of view. It is possible to say that in some dream states, or trance states, or states of shock, or of exhaustion, the action of this second world may become evident. These states are often referred to in literature as movements in which "time stands still" and "one is not oneself." The former saying refers to the abeyance of the coordinates of the first world, the latter to the suspension of the "identity" associated with the first world, that is, personality. Associated with this world and our perception of its action are the incursions of unpredictable but significant events. The first world is ruled by the predictable, but the second may act through a rupture in the predictable order, a flash (the image used more often than any other for a moment of insight), a hazard, or a failure. "When we live automatically," says Anthony Blake, speaking of the first world, "we simply repeat what has been, and we live in a state in which our future is exactly the same as our past".[19] "It is very interesting to wake up from this state and to realize that nothing on this level can lead to anything... suddenly in the middle of the ["predict-able"] universe something comes out of nowhere which doesn't fit in. [...] Something emerges independent of the causal stream of the past."[20]

This new state is characteristic of mediations from the world of the creative imagination, what Jung called the world of archetypes, which were important to his analytic method because their appearance (or a training in which their appearance could be encouraged) effectively illustrates that the coordinates of the first world, which psychology calls conditioning, can lapse to bring about a change in the human's state of consciousness. As we have seen from the poets' and mystics' remarks, to be conversant with the other worlds is actually the "natural state"[21] for man, and imprisonment in the first world—living in it as though it were the only world—is an unnatural state. Jung's celebrated synchronistic events, evidence for him as for Arthur Koestler, of an "acausal connecting principle,"[22] are actually the second world manifesting in the first world. Anthony Blake refers to precisely such events as "a more synchronous experience, which means an experience relatively free of the disordering effects of time and space, but often idolized as the world of the paranormal; [...] a world of natural relevance, relatively free of the conditions of separation and succession. Names, things, and personalities vanish as discrete entities."[23] As Koestler put it, "the integrative potentials of life seem to include the capacity of producing pseudo-causal effects, of bringing about a confluential event without bothering, so to speak, to employ physical agencies."[24]

This "second" world has many names, a brief and selective list of which will give some idea of the variety of traditions which have identified it:

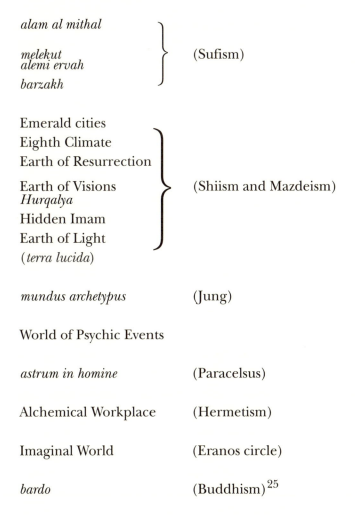

alam al mithal

melekut
alemi ervah   (Sufism)

barzakh

Emerald cities
Eighth Climate
Earth of Resurrection

Earth of Visions   (Shiism and Mazdeism)
Hurqalya
Hidden Imam
Earth of Light
(*terra lucida*)

mundus archetypus   (Jung)

World of Psychic Events

astrum in homine   (Paracelsus)

Alchemical Workplace   (Hermetism)

Imaginal World   (Eranos circle)

bardo   (Buddhism)[25]

It is known in all these traditions as the world in which "Spirits are corporealized and bodies subtilized"; in a phrase which

Dr. Johnson is perhaps better known for coining than for having understood, a world, like the poetic world, "which embodies sentiment and animates matter." It is thus an intermediary world, an isthmus (*barzakh*) which relates to the worlds on either side of it, relates, that is, to the first world of everyday life (by the means of images and symbols) and to the third world (by means of such symbols' not being the dependents of the physical world so much as recipients of the powers or intelligences expressed by the third world). The second world is the medium (*barzakh* also means medium) through which the creative impulses enter from a yet higher world into the present, and have the opportunity to actualize.

We said the first world was a world that could be likened to an always predictable action, running on the fixed plan of past expectation to present function, what the Romantics called the "dull round," the "lethargy of custom." This world becomes creative only when creative powers break in, *via* the second world (dream, shock, flash, intuitive awakening) from the third world. The second world is, then, a medium of communication from the third world to the first. Such communication is known also under the name *kairos*, or "auspiciousness," connected, interestingly, with the incidence of the "dharmakaya light" in the Buddhist tradition; a light which is sensed in the second world when a dynamic potential is felt breaking through onto a situation till then determined by mechanism and habit.[26] That light is what establishes a connection with the third world.

What is the third world? Asking this brings us even further from the laws which govern the physical world, laws which influence language, and maintain (through the activity of the second world) contact with dreams and trance states. This third world can be conceived as the world of powers, of integrative potentials, of intelligences, the light world, the world of glory (*Xvarnah*), the world of spiritual determinations, the

jabarut, or *âlemi imkan*, the first intelligence, first manifestation
(*ta'ayyun awwal*), the world of seminal reasons, first light.[27] It
can be glimpsed in the proposition that "the power of seeing is
there before the physical eye is formed."[28] Goethe states: "the
eye owes its existence to light. From a [...] sensory apparatus,
[...] light has called forth, produced for itself, an organ like
unto itself; thus the eye was formed by light, of light and for
light, so that the inner light might come to contact with the
outer light."[29] That description has forerunners in the *Zohar*
and other traditions. "This is the primal light which God made.
It is the light of the eye."[30] It is known as the world of latencies
or lights, as it is from this world that creative impulses come
into the human situation, noticeable as a potential presenting
itself out of the future, not out of the past.[31] This is the reason
for the unpredictable nature of experiences of the second
world (Imagination), whose impulse is from the third world; its
influence is to draw what in the human world can respond to
creativity (because it *is* creativity) through the worlds back to its
source. These impulses as they "exist" or pre-exist in the third
world are free from the laws of the second and first worlds.

In the sense that the determinations in the third world are
not those of the first world, which is customarily called existence, it is possible to say that the third world, in the event that
it contacts a human being, gives that being a sense of non-
existence: "cracks come in the shell that covers us," writes J. G.
Bennett; "we begin to see things differently. At first it may be
very painful; but it helps us to put away the illusions of our
somethingness,"[32] a somethingness which only has meaning
in the first world (and, to an extent, in the second).

When the potentials of the third world are made evident to
someone experiencing the second-world state, the result nar-
rated in the first world is a veridical dream. When someone is
in the second world state without its being an intermediary for
a communication from the third world, the result is a neutral

dream-life, and, at extremes, madness or psychosis, a chaos of imagination. This is agreed in the esoteric schools and will be shown to be precisely repeated in the schemes of the Romantic poets.[33]

When the fourth world enters into the account we are at the ultimate.[34] So the very thought *that it enters* or that "we are" anywhere, is a gross inaccuracy. Wittgenstein refers to the fourth world when he says *"Worüber man nicht sprechen kann, darüber muß man schweigen."*[35] Here we "arrive" at, if we had ever departed, the Non-Being of the Buddhists and Taoists, the *ghayb* or *lahut* of the Sufis, the non-predicated reality of David Bohm's implicate order.[36]

> Being in itself is non-entified, and consequently non-delimited, inarticulated, without name, attribute or quality. So it cannot be described in positive terms.[37]

Some idea can, in the right situation, be gained from hints like this. Also, etymologically, the word *absolute* suggests what is being referred to. *Absolved, absolute,* means *without solution,* that is, essence without solution or dilution. Water assumes the color of the vessel containing it, according to the Sufi proverb; this relates to the "colors" assumed in the *solution* and *densification* of essence, Absolute Being, into its devolutions and delimitations. Peter Lamborn Wilson offers an extraordinary insight into the ultimate paradox, which is the constant focus of philosophy, religion, and poetry when it is taken to the highest level:

> How do we know that Being is nonentified? Because every entity that has being, everything that exists, is a delimitation of Being as such. We say "the horse *is,* the tree *is,* Tom *is,* the devil *is,* God *is.*" The common measure is *isness.* Nor is this *isness* a mental construct. Rather, it is the fundamental

nature of all things. Each entity, each thing, each existent, is one possibility of "entification," hidden within the nature of sheer Being, just as each colour is one possibility of coloration possessed by the very essence of pure light.[38]

This sheerness, ab-solution, non-entification is what is said, *faute de mieux*, of the fourth world, of which nothing can be said. Contact with it on any of its levels above the first world thus enacts, or appears to enact, an annihilation or extinction in the first world, and effects the explosion, or collapse, of language. This is what all mystics and metaphysicians, the Tibetan meditation masters and Wittgenstein alike, salute in the move to silence. And such silence is the destination, if we can so call it, of the sacred grammar explored in chapter 2. It is the Reality, the fourth world, on which all meditation is predicated, from which it proceeds, and at which it appears to aim.

The fourth world also appears to be the Reality on which is predicated some of the greatest poetry every written. In what has become known as the "Skylark Ode," Shelley speaks not only of—but addresses directly as *thou*—the Source, and the impulse toward it in all manifestation.

The bird/spirit, carefully spared definition—"bird thou never wert"—is identified with the second world and the worlds above, "Heaven, or near it";

> Higher and still higher
> From the Earth thou springest
> […]
> Singing still dost soar,
> And soaring ever singest.

This "scorner of the ground" is also "a cloud of fire," an "unbodied joy whose race"—the journey in existence—"is just begun." As native of the third world and higher, the race just begun is the journey of the descent; seen from the point of view of a descended being, the race is the "ascent" which the bird, in its very physique a symbol of convection, has begun.

Like the third and fourth worlds, indeed like the *haqq*, "thou" is for Shelley "unseen." "We hardly see, we feel, that it is there." Responding to the influences of the second, third, and fourth worlds,

> All the Earth and air
> With thy voice is loud.

That is to say, the upper worlds are expressed through their permeation of the lower; it is the tropism of the lower toward the upper, its prayer, which manifestation brings about, or which, rather, is manifestation's sole cause.

The First Principle, Source, the *haqq*, the Unique, is something to which no comparison can admit a second. "What thou art we know not; What is most like thee?" asks the poet, at the same time knowing, as Rumi did, that no metaphor (direct comparison of one thing with another) can illustrate that "You did not throw when you threw"; Shelley gives no reply to his own question except a suggestion (twice repeated) of one time-honored metaphor which is allowed even the most rigorous practitioner of non-dual awareness, the rain of divine mercy.

> From rainbow clouds there flow not
> Drops so bright to see
> As from thy presence showers a rain of melody.

Interestingly, and with metaphysical precision, Shelley collapses the existential language function by denial of the metaphor—there *flow* *not* from rainbow clouds such drops—echoing the similar collapse in the statement of unity called the *Shahadah*, "There is no Divinity save the Divinity." At the same time, in a supreme act of tact, "thy presence" is not grammatically subject to the earlier denial, and this is fitting because *thy* presence is the presence of Reality, not limited to a bird or a word. "Bird thou never wert."

The concealment of the Real, of the fourth world, an ineffability causing it to be known to the Sufis as *Ghayb* (Unseen) is indicated by Shelley's images of the maiden in the secret tower, the glow-worm "unbeholden," "screen[ed] from view"; the rose

> embowered
> In its own green leaves.

Indications of the bird's unseen presence in the second, third and fourth worlds occur to the poet, and show in his avoidance of the time scheme of the first world of space-time. The "profuse strains," the "overflowed Heaven" (itself a traditional form of the Holy Effusion of the Sufis or the Divine Effluence of Böhme) are "unpremeditated," "unbidden," and both expressions suggest the supraterrestrial origin of the bidding and the "premeditation." In other words, the Source which bids, which gives the command or effuses through love, is identified with the *thou* whom Shelley praises in his poem. Unbidden, unpremeditated, because the interventions of the upper worlds—in sacred time experiences, psychic events breaking in on the first world, the things sometimes that "we mortals dream"—are not commanded by us but can only be received, as rays by a mirror or water by earth.

It is this order of being which praise itself, as a mode of speech, expresses. Shelley shows its full understanding here, speaking of the ideal human state:

———

If we could scorn
Hate, and pride and fear;
If we were things born
Not to shed a tear,
I know not how thy joy we ever could come near.

Whatever the degree of human enlightenment, the order never reverses. The Most High never changes places, even though the bird's flight aspires to it. Thus and in the same way the white light of the Buddhist *dharmakaya*[39] is filtered in the first and second worlds, to prevent the visionary from being blinded. This filtering could be said to be the sole reason for Shelley's, the Platonists' and the Sufis' doctrine of the veils. The same filtering action is noticed by Shelley in different but breathtaking terms in "Adonais," his elegy on the death of Keats:

Heaven's light forever shines, Earth's shadows fly;
Life, like a dome of many-coloured glass,
Stains the white radiance of eternity,
Until Death trample it to fragments.—Die,
If thou wouldst be with that which thou dost seek!
Follow where all is fled!—Rome's azure sky,
Flowers, ruins, statues, music, words, are weak
The glory they transfuse with fitting truth to speak.

In case the reader of the "Skylark Ode" should move toward judging Shelley himself, as so many seem to do, as a "scorner of the ground," it is worth remembering how strong a grasp of the first world he shows in his poem, which is mostly trying to invoke the soaring or upward current. The indices of the first world state, its gravitational "stickiness" and its peculiar time awareness, are clearly established in the phrases "shadow of annoyance," "languor," "love's sad satiety," tears, and in this brief, virtually perfect consonance with Buddhist and Sufi teaching on the false self of personality:

> We look before and after,
> And pine for what is not.

Before and after refers to the desire which clings to the past and hankers for future success, entirely asleep to the Great Present Moment, which is the only maker of any real future and healer of past wrongs, the moment which is the crack in the confines of the first world through which the influence of the further worlds can penetrate. We pine for this past and future, for "what is not," because it is not here and now. What is, said Krishnamurti, is now. According to Blake, "eternity [is] in an hour."

The invocatory and esoteric tradition in which Shelley's poem is composed could not be better exemplified than by the twice-made request for teaching, which Shelley addresses to *thou* in the second half of the ode:

> Teach us, sprite or bird,
> What sweet thoughts are thine.
> [...]
> Teach me half the gladness...

Praise is really only for that which is *beyond measure*. This is the order of the praise Shelley offers here to the Bird's aspirations, and to the Encourager which is the spirit's unseen, unspeakable, unwriteable presence.

> Better than all measures
> Of delightful sound,
> Better than all treasures
> That in books are found.

This, then, concludes a brief account of the worlds as it is contained in the esoteric tradition and realized in the form of

---

poetry. Several points need to be borne in mind when think-ing along the lines suggested. First, each world is englobed and permeated by the next, so it is in some ways misleading to see the worlds as though they are rooms in a house. Second, the persistent conditioning of awareness by the first world means that its state is by far the most "statistically common" of the states connected with the worlds. But it is possible for the experience of the first world either to be an experience unin-fluenced by any higher order (unenlightened experience), or for it to be instinct with the permeations of the higher worlds, and to the degree of its knowledge of "whence it is contin-gent," it is enlightened.[40] But on few occasions in the world of time, the first world, does the enlightened person appear any different from any other person. The prophetic intimation says: "Do not look for me in yourself, you would be going to futile pains. But do not seek me either outside of you, you would not succeed. Discriminate between me and thee, for you will not see me, you will see only your hexeity."[41] This is the key to why mystical gnosis can on no account be equated with "pantheism." Henry Corbin puts it thus:

> The Divine Being reveals himself to us only in the config-urations of the theophanic imagination, which gives effec-tive reality to those divine names whose sadness yearned for concrete beings in whom to invest their activity.

The "hexeity" is equivalent to the "names" Corbin mentions. These are peculiar to the third of the worlds, the light world, and it is *from* there, but in the second world, that a contempla-tive receives the contact or initiation sought.[42] This is what is implied in the metaphysical dialogue of theophany (explored in chapter 2), according to the Sufi theosophical dictum: "He who knows himself knows his lord."[43] "God is not the God of the dogmatic definitions who can subsist without any relation to the individual. Rather it is the God who can know himself only 'through the knowledge that I have of him, because it is the knowledge that he has of me.'"[44] If we recall J. G. Bennett's words quoted at the beginning, we will see that he and Corbin are speaking of the same gnosis from different directions: "although it is difficult to grasp at first exposure, once people have learned how to relate it to their own experience, it becomes possible for them to understand and talk about things which otherwise would be too elusive."[45] According then to its nature, the hexeity or name devolves into the first world as action or disposition.

Thirdly, and very importantly for an understanding of the way the poets moved toward their comprehension of the human condition, once the first world is left behind, so to speak, all notions of time become irrelevant. There are many sayings which intimate this abeyance of time, one of them being that of the Sufis that "[before creation] God was in a state such that there was nothing with Him [fourth world]. Even at this moment He is still so.";[46] and another is the metaphysics of the Breaths, according to which creation is originated and annihilated at every moment.[47] This esoteric science expresses the radical change in time which accompanies consciousness in the second, third, and fourth worlds, and it is echoed today in quantum theory.[48] Another traditional expression of the change in time experienced in the worlds beyond the first world is the Quranic proverb concerning the night journey (*miraj*) of the Prophet Mohammed, which indicates the entire event took place in the time it takes for a glass to fall from table to floor. Another Quranic verse mentions the same rupture of the accustomed time of the first world, in its description of the divine devolution from the fourth world to the first:

> Our affairs are accomplished in as short a time as a wink or even in much shorter time.[49]

For William Blake, too, this "ending of time" had a special meaning and was his esoteric interpretation of the traditional Apocalyptic stories, as well as being a radically different interpretation of ordinary life:

> The hours of folly are measured by the clock, but of wisdom no clock can measure.

> As our perceptions vary, objects seem to vary.

> Whenever an Individual rejects Error and Embraces Truth, then a last Judgement passes upon that Individual.[50]

And it was no different for the Sufi Al Ghazzali: "We all know that time has no absolute existence. It is only a form of our knowledge, of our nature, as related to the experience of nature outside."[51] On such entry to higher worlds as the creative imagination makes possible, "eternity" can indeed occupy an hour. Or even less. William Blake was in no doubt:

> The world of Imagination is the world of eternity.

> Every Time less than the pulsation of an artery
> Is equal in its period and value to Six Thousand Years
> For in this period the Poet's Work is done, and all the
>   Great
> Events of Time start forth & are conceived in
>   such a period,
> Within a moment, a Pulsation of the Artery.[52]

6

THE JOURNEYS

And we are put on earth a little space
That we may learn to bear the beams of love.

—BLAKE

The man of gnosis should know his place of beginning
and his place of return; where he came from and where
he is going.

—MUHYIDDIN IBN 'ARABI

WITH SOME IDEA IN MIND as to the nature of the worlds opened up by the Active Imagination, it remains to explore how the path from world to world is realized and imaged in the metaphysics of the journey—from home, into exile, and home again. Esoteric training itself, the world over, is called a journey or path, and its image and meaning, like those of the primal phenomena, have penetrated into every outward aspect of life and language, leave aside permeating the inner.

A journey, or *the* journey, is implicated in nearly everything that is said and done, as in every organic process. The journey is, for instance, implied in what takes place between a human's birth and death, and, likewise, implied at any point during life when the question is asked, after an experience or in face of one coming: is this a step forward, or simply more of the same?

From earliest times birth and death have been seen in their *Urphänomenal* aspect in the scriptural phrases about "being born again" (Christian) and "die before you die" (Sufi). The metaphysics of the journey, like all true metaphysics, apply at

---

any level. All doctrines of rebirth imply it, but, as we shall see, it does not require a literal doctrine of reincarnation.

For the mystics and the Romantic poets, the journey between birth and death is only one "half" of the affair. (And even *half* is a misleading word, as we will shortly see. For every journey measured in time, in the first world, there are many journeys unmeasured, but, so to speak, happening at each moment.) The complementary journey, that between death and birth, offers another perspective, which Plato's writings made as clear as it perhaps could be made.[1]

Numerous myths depict the "descent of the soul," Plato's archetype of the journey and his doctrine of *anamnesis,* or re-collection of past lives. That there are so many myths variant on the same theme means that none can be mentioned as definitive, but the myth of Cupid and Psyche can be singled out, along with the myth of the Phoenix, and that of Orpheus. What will be concerning us here is the constitution which all these myths share in their various accounts of the journey, accounts amongst which there is "divergence, to be sure, but seldom contradiction."[2]

In all the accounts Eastern and Western, the journey moves from the upper world to the underworld, from the world of light to the world of darkness, and back again. It is immaterial whether the order is reversed—from lower to upper, and back again—because the journey is the same whatever stage of it happens to claim attention. From the point of view of Earth, the journey starts at birth; from the point of view of the upper worlds it starts before birth or after death, in those worlds. The variance of point of view does not affect the journey, but sim-ply reminds us of the profound reciprocity of origin and desti-nation, and the relationship thus instanced between the relative and the absolute.

As was the case with the four worlds, a brief rehearsal of the journey is necessary, distilled from a large number of accounts.

As always in the esoteric philosophy, it is not a simple matter to name the protagonist in the journey. It has been variously called the soul, the monad, the human being, the angel, the immortal spirit, the reincarnating entity, the spark, and so forth, each of which designations corresponds to the contours of the legend or tradition which it belongs to; let us say that it changes names as it moves through cultures, states, and worlds, but the meaning of the journey is precisely that there is one traveller at once undergoing a process, and contributing to it. "The seeker is the instrument of the knowledge sought," according to the proverb.

Let us assume the traveller "starts" in the heavens, or rather that this is the place where our summary description finds him or her. The traveller is in the upper region, the fourth world, where there is no existence as we perceive it; he or she is in the world of non-delimited being, or pure light.

non-delimited being

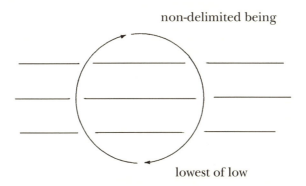

lowest of low

Owing to a mysterious impulse—many traditions say God's wish to know himself in a "mirror"—the traveller begins the "descent" into the worlds of potentials, ideas, archetypal delimitations, and conditions, and then into the "solidifications" of the foregoing: the world of objects. This "outward" journey, through the right hemisphere on the diagram, is known as the descent. The position of "the lowest of the low"[3] does not necessarily indicate moral lowness, but ontological lowness, the extension of the absolute into its furthest possible materiality. In this state the human being is found entering the physical world at birth, having gone through an experience of "amnesiac" erasure of knowledge of his previous states, a forgetting which Greek mythology images in the dipping in the waters of Lethe, which Plato describes in his doctrine of *anamnesis* as the only way the traveller can bear entering the earth-state. That this forgetting takes place is very important in making sense of the entire mystical journey. In the higher worlds the physical body is/was not present. This earth-state then is proverbially called the "vale of tears"; what Keats alternatively calls the "vale of soul-making"; what the Buddhists refer to as the world of suffering (*samsara, dukkha*). The very word "vale" that is so entrenched in our clichéd designations of life on Earth has its root in the visualization of a diagram of *descent* (possibly from the metaphysical mountain [Qaf, Kailash, Meru, Abora], as mentioned in chapter 7).

And hidden in these two proverbial phrases is the cause and symptom of the start of the next "half" of the journey, upward from the "underworld" to the higher worlds, and back to the absolute. In the esoteric tradition, tears, the "water of the eyes," symbols of suffering, are the very mark of the innate motivation of the traveller to return to where he came from. They are, in the language of the Abrahamic tradition, the "seal of the covenant";[4] suggesting the same is also the "esoteric psychology" of tears: we frequently fail to find a direct explanation for shedding tears. Disregarding the obvious incidents which might promote them, the other occasions do suggest that the cause is hidden. The hidden motivations for tears preoccupied Tennyson all his life.[5] According to the metaphysics of the esoteric journey, tears, like suffering, are dim reminders of what we have not entirely forgotten during the dipping in Lethe or *amnesis* of incarnation. Jung has described in some of his patients a greater or lesser consent or agreement "to the fact of having been born," and this would correlate to a greater or lesser capacity to erase the memories of a pre-birth state.

We are at the heart of Buddhism, too, here, as well as of the Western tradition; we see in the circular image the wheel of suffering which the soul longs to free itself from. It could be said that suffering in itself, and coming to terms with it, is the "push" or shock needed to start the traveller on the "path of return," which is the other half of the journey that began with the descent of the soul from the divine world to the world of time and space, from the Great Unknowable (*ghayb i mutlaq*) through the degrees of knowledge afforded by "sojourns" in the four worlds.

Nothing is fixed in this scheme, except the orientation, which is always clear, and reflected in all the other conditions or phenomena of being. Thus, although we may say from a certain angle that the incarnation-state is the furthest removed from the divinity, perhaps the most "hardened," nevertheless the equilibrium of organisms is delicately poised in the complex "dance" of the four elements, particularly those of "fire" and "water," so that the living being can at any moment, so to speak, "dry up" (dehydration) or "drown," decay, in excessive moisture (corruption). This formulation is the secret of the Chinese alchemists and Taoists, who, like Heraclitus, speak of even the material world as constant flow.

The path of soul-descent is related to the behavior of water, the water-principle (see chapter 7) whose cycle encompasses heating, vaporization, condensation, precipitation, and collecting/outspreading on the ground. Blake, Böhme, Swedenborg, and others in the esoteric tradition characteristically relate this water principle involved in the descent into incarnation with the fluids of human sexual exchange and the amniotic fluid in which the embryo is supported. Compare Christ's words, concerning "birth of water and the spirit."

Conversely, the fire-principle is one of the forces which carries the soul upward, initiating the path of return, which death of the physically descended "water" organism automatically induces but which may begin—owing to the human faculty of reflexivity—before the moment of physical death. Here the prophetic axiom of Sufism, "Die before you die," becomes relevant, as do Christ's words "Except you die to be born again...."

Re-birth in the spirit is what folk tradition recalls in distinguishing *the once-born* from *the twice-born*. It is *anamnesis*—remembering where "you" come from and where, therefore, you are certain to return, given the principle of the wholeness or unity in which this entire metaphysics from East to West subsists. And as mentioned, the fire-principle is involved in the turn from the earth. At this point the soul "takes wing," begins to attract and sympathize with the bird-like capacities and tendencies mentioned in chapter 7, but it does not fly out of its sphere altogether. If divorced entirely from any trace of "moisture," it would shoot up into "Lucifer," or else suffer the fate of Icarus's journey, and is bound to be a failure because, like a forced plant, it has failed to observe the order and speed of the path taken in its fullest sense. This "holding-up" or arrest of the swiftness of the fire-principle by the water-principle during human life is one of the root meanings of compassion for life, the highest principle of the Buddhist sainthood. For to protect the existing and growing organisms—be they plant, animal, or human—means in itself to hold onto life long enough to let this development happen, whereas the ruthlessly "aspiring" soul, devoid of compassion, would quit the wheel of suffering as quickly as possible regardless, because it considered itself independent, even separate from its kind.

Is the very meaning of compassion not the underlying reason for Keats's so marked interest in the Zoroastrian version of the path of descent and return, to whose earthly installment he gave the name "vale of *soul-making*"?[6] It suggests that there is a meaning or a "constructive" interpretation to be found in the precarious fire-water balance that organic life can be said to be maintained in. In Keats's phrase, as in Blake's "learning to bear the beams of love," there is a clear suggestion that the earth-state is a state of education, not an anomalous hell-time or a meaningless torment.

The invocations by the Romantic poets, and the mystics, of the "water of generation," of sexuality, are important here, given the extent to which its manifestations dominated the living of Romantics and still dominate human culture in ways which defy dismissal. There is no such thing as "free sex," it may be interesting to suggest, since whatever is benefited from as a means of flight from the "prison of self" must be paid for with compassion, which is "freedom from self" in a different key. Value, here, is not the purely mercantile currency of financial outlay but the giving of compassionate attention to living beings, the extension, possibly, of the "luminous cloud" mentioned by Coleridge which must "issue forth from the soul" and "envelop the earth" in order that it may be felt to be living;[7] this again brings us to the Buddhist eightfold path, which subsists, be it said, without the need of the kind of theocratic state-machine which has earned the Western organized religions such increasing disrepute.

The recondite theme of a sexual-esoteric alchemy could be illuminated somewhat by suggesting that Shelley's was a fire-nature, almost obsessed with heat, light, wind, the upward impulsion of convection currents, the artificial manufacture of sparks;[8] and that the enormous force of the progress his "ascent" made with these means could not be paid for by him in the form of compassion, hence the abandonment and death of many of his partners and children. There can be no question of making a moral judgement here, given the extraordinary complexity of the elements in Shelley's personal life, but what can be ventured is an estimate of the balance of alchemical principles, from a knowledge of which the hieratic arts invited self-knowledge as a process which any individual, complex or simple, could undergo. It is nothing other than the path of return, according to these sources, which is contacted when any lover, parent, traveller, mendicant, scholar, scientist, poet, warrior, comes to recognize the truth of their experience at its apogee. *Initiation is obtained from life*, say the alchemists and esotericists, not from abstraction from life. Perhaps the greatest misunderstanding to which the spiritual ways have been exposed during the nineteenth and twentieth centuries is the idea that these considerations of human origin and destination have nothing to do with life as we experience it from day to day. On the contrary, the scene of the journey, for all who undergo it, is here, and it is now.

The liberation which the traveller seeks is not liberation from life but from forgetfulness—a forgetfulness which is called life by those determined to see no further until some catastrophe, major (like war) or minor (like a shock, a veridical dream, or a mid-life crisis) breaches the wall of Habit,[9] the "lethargy of custom" (according to Coleridge) or "film of familiarity" (according to Shelley), which "obscures from us the wonder of our being."[10]

As there are two births so there are two deaths, the death of ego and the death of the body. These may coincide, or they may not. But what is remarked upon by many traditions is that if the ego death does not happen in the present incarnation, the traveller must incarnate again to "learn to bear the beams of love" through still more experiences, many of them designed to reveal the ego's non-existence, which is after all the only condition in which love is said to be able to realize itself in human life.

Unless the fundamental nature of mind is recognized in the intermediate state following death and preceding conception, the mental continuum, influenced by its

114

accumulated predispositions, is ineluctably drawn once more into re-embodiment in an appropriate physical environment.[11]

Thus is imagined the constant stream of souls entering and leaving the place of manifestation, the Earth, the first world as described in chapter 5. According to the Buddhists, those for whom the false personality is dissolved in one incarnation via "the accelerated path" are then free but still may return in another incarnation (that of the *bodhisattva*) to assist those who are still bound.

All the images of *exile* occurring in mysticism and in Romantic poetry have their roots in the metaphysical journey we have been contemplating here from various angles. The difference between temporary habitation and home is imaged, as is the journey, over and over again:

Be in this world as if you are a traveller... Be always a passer-by, for this is not home.[12]

All this edifice [the world of time and space] is there to announce and denounce his captivity to the human being, to stimulate him to awaken to consciousness of his origin. The magnificent dome becomes a cage, a prison from which he must escape.

It is by awakening to the feeling of being a stranger that the gnostic's soul discovers *where* it is and at the same time forebodes *whence it* comes and *whither* it returns.[13]

> ... trailing clouds of glory do we come
> From God, who is our home.
>   Though inland far we be,
> Our souls have sight of that immortal sea

> Which brought us hither,
> Can in a moment travel thither ...[14]

Perhaps the wonder of the business, certainly the heart of the initiation, comes at that turning point (*metanoia*) between the state of ego consciousness endured hitherto and the beginning of the metaphysical journey; for as Corbin has so vividly described in his book on Avicenna's metaphysics it is only at the very point of realizing one's exile, that one finds out one can "go home" at all. The exile who does not experience himself as an exile is not exiled, but instead feels at home. As Wordsworth puts it, "Earth fills her lap with pleasures of her own."[15] It is only upon the realization that one is a stranger that the primary invitation comes to travel, or more precisely, to continue the journey whose arrested state one took (in "sleep and forgetting") to be the real world or the only state. It is this turning point from "sleep to waking" which formed the core teaching of the Russian mystic Gurdjieff.[16]

The *process* of invitation and response is one we should watch closely for its correspondences with the themes opened up in the previous essays in this gnosiology. For the traveller on the journey, the soul whose journey this essay has been pursuing, is, when outside the time-bound sphere of the first world, not subject to the constraints any more than to the designations which the first world imposes with its word, *journey.* He is, in the third and fourth worlds, at once his beginning and his end. So, on the incarnated traveller's awakening to the possibility of his return, he perceives, according to Corbin, an *inviter.*

> At the moment when the soul discovers itself to be a stranger and alone in a world formerly familiar, a *personal* figure appears on its horizon, a figure that announces itself to the soul *personally* because it sympathizes with the soul's most intimate depths.[17]

Compare Coleridge, viewing the "horizon" represented by land- and sky-scape:

> An obscure feeling as if that phenomen[on] were the dim awakening of a truth of my inner nature... In looking at objects of Nature... I seem to be seeking, as it were *asking* for, a symbolical language for something within me that already and forever exists.[18]

Corbin again:

> The soul discovers itself to be the earthly counterpart of another being with which it forms a totality dual in structure.[19]

This seeming contradiction between dual and total being dissolves if we admit to living in four worlds at once, not just in one world (see chapter 5). Few thinkers have been as clear as Corbin on this meaning of invitation in the presence of the Unity of the Sole Existent, though it is reflected in all the traditions of which he writes, and comes via those traditions to the Romantics (across varying routes).[20]

> The two elements of this *dualitude* may be called the ego and the self, or the transcendent celestial self and the earthly self, or by still other names. It is from this transcendent self that the soul originates in the past of metahistory: this self had become strange to it while the soul slumbered in the world of ordinary consciousness; but it ceases to be strange to it at the moment when the soul in turn feels itself a stranger in this world.[21]

This is the reason why, according to Wordsworth, "our souls [which] have sight of that immortal sea / which brought us hither / can in a moment travel thither"—because it is the *soul,* denizen of the soul world, of the *mithal* or Active Imagination world, which *joins* (*barzakh*) "this" world and the "next." This fact explains the apparent duality of the seeker (traveller) and the Guide. They seem to be separate, but are actually one and the same yet in different worlds. The figure of the Guide, heavenly counterpart of the soul, says Corbin,

> manifests itself to the soul only at the dawn, the "sunrise" of the soul's perfect individuation, its integration, because only then is its relation to the divine individualized.[22]

Consequently, the dawn-light and crepuscular imagery beloved of the Romantics, for instance in Wordsworth's "Immortality Ode," is anything but a coincidental ornament. This dawn is the *Ishraq* (light of glory)[23] of the ancient theosophists quite as much as Wordsworth's "clouds of glory" or our "life's Star [Paracelsus' *astrum in homine*] which hath elsewhere its setting."[24] This dawning is the meeting across the horizon, imaged in chapter 3 of this book as the *metaphysical conversation.* But here we see it in terms of the *whence* and *whither* of the traveller's journey. In the language of esoteric metaphysics, the meaning of the word destination, the *whither* of the journey, is where one is "destined" to go.[25]

What is it, then, that gives the "push" which eventuates this moment of meeting? this divine sunrise, the appearing of one's "celestial guide" or life's star?

It is, I suggest, a combination of two factors, indeed, their intersection, one might say. The first factor is "readiness," an openness to the possibility of integration should a moment be favorable. In the words of Ibn 'Arabi:

> concerning the existents in all their differentiation[:] they are the manifestation of God (*al Haqq*) in the loci of manifestation [...] *in keeping with the preparednesses of these possible things.*[26]

He who discloses Himself is one entity in himself, but the disclosures differ because of the preparednesses of the loci.[27]

As the Sufis say, precisely to the degree that the mirror is polished will the divine light reflect in it, but only to that degree.[28] It is in that context that the way of the heart is also called the *Polishing*.

The readiness is one factor, a full outline of which is probably more appropriate to a manual of mystical guidance than a gnosiology of Romanticism, but it is an indispensable condition for the incident which is described as the metaphysical meeting, or initiation, or being "given a push."

A second factor is the accumulation and action of sufficient psychic energy to breach the confines of the habitual world, the time-space-matter-dimensions of the *nasut*, the corporeal world or first world, a breach graphically implied in the proverbial formulation "earth-shattering experience" which is applied to states far more individual, personal, and private than its surface meaning, "global destruction," might suggest.

Such energy is manufactured, to use a clumsy expression, in the second world, or world of imagination, and its action in the first instance is rather like the breach of a wall by water force and the submerging in itself of all that the water meets. It is in this sense that at a certain time the "oceanic feeling" of mystical language finds some application, however misleading it has proved to be in other contexts.

However, drowning "in water" is not loss of awareness but on the contrary an enormous boost to awareness, when it succeeds. Corbin says:

A powerful source of psychic energy is necessary if the imaginative activity… is to be capable of creating, beyond common expressions and outworn or interchangeable symbolisms, a sufficient field of inner freedom for the

---

manifestation of the image of this self that existed before the earthly condition and expects to survive it.[29]

This "image" is the mediation of "the face you had before you were born," which is the treasure the Zen koan challenges the meditator to find.[30] Again the teachers of meditation and the Romantic poets enter the same ground, ground which was explored in terms of meditation in chapter 3. The "sufficient field of inner freedom" is created by the cultivation and supersession of meditative states, in which one is nearer to the world of the Imagination, the second world.

> The event will take place in a mental vision, a "waking dream"—in a state, as our visionaries always define it… "intermediate between waking and sleep."[31]

Elémire Zolla draws attention to just such a field of experience in his description of *samadhi*, the state of pure contemplation.

> It is precisely when unconstrained and egoless that minds grasp truth in a flash. *Samadhi* is unification and quietude, the contrary of torpor, even if it might sometimes look like coma. Stupor and the swoon of an in-gathering mind are worlds apart, but people conditioned to appreciate tense, deliberate, cramped modes of life tend to mistake one for the other.[32]

It is not difficult to see how categorically the Romantics turned their backs on the deliberate, tense, and cramped mode.

> And even the motion of our human blood
> Almost suspended, we are laid asleep
> In body, and become a living soul:

While which an eye made quiet by the power
Of harmony, and the deep power of joy,
We see into the life of things.

(Wordsworth)

Ah! slowly sink
Behind the western ridge, thou glorious Sun!
Shine in the slant beams of the sinking orb,
Ye purple heath-flowers! richlier burn, ye clouds!
Live in the yellow light, ye distant groves!
And kindle, thou blue ocean! So my friend
Struck with deep joy may stand, as I have stood.
Silent with swimming sense; yea, gazing round
On the wide landscape, gaze till all doth seem
Less gross than bodily; and of such hues
As veil the Almighty Spirit, when yet he makes
Spirits perceive his presence.

(Coleridge)

Many Romantic poets turned their writing to this *samadhi,* but few as well as Coleridge at his best. They did it to invite just such events as Zolla and Corbin point to.

> The inwardness and surrender of *samadhi* are the conditions of rapid realizations, of lucky, dashing interventions [...] Through utter amalgamation, *samadhi realizes the essence of things and events, by feeling itself at their root, as their creator.*[33]

At such times, the path of return is complete for the moment, for the first world no longer holds sway over our perceptions. Knowledge of the outer world has been returned to its source.

7

NATURE IN THE SCIENCE OF BEING

Symbol and Phenomenon

Isn't it striking that, as soon as one dreams of images of high cosmicity, the images of fire, water, or the bird, [one] has evidence, by reading the poets, of an entirely new activity of the creative imagination?

—BACHELARD

In the beginning, boundless compassion is like a seed; it becomes as water and manure in the middle, and as ripe fruit at the end.

—ACHARYA CHANDRAKIRTI

MENTION HAS BEEN MADE, in chapter 5, of the ontological implications of the metamorphosis of insects, and the manner in which, say, the developing butterfly reflects human transformation, or being drawn through the worlds, presences, or states. But the essence of these analogies is that, since they give us an insight into the nature of *analogy*, an even deeper insight can be reached than the one assigned to analogy by linguists and the science of signs (structuralism). The reason Goethe, Novalis, Shelley, to name only three of the Romantics with this interest, studied the analogies was that they were an induction into a more direct knowledge, or knowing, than the term *analogy* would first imply; they were an example of Intelligence[1] in contemplation and realization of itself. According to Bachelard, in the contemplation (or as Owen Barfield put it, participation) of these phenomena, the divine devolutions explained in the treatises of metaphysicians could be witnessed, not in the abstract, but in living fact, that is, not disregarding the biological continuum.[2] The Romantic philosophy of nature has its basis in this principle, enunciated earlier by the mystics such as Böhme in Europe, Rumi in the Middle East, and much earlier by the Taoists in the Far East. It affords a direct knowledge of the *process* of the self-manifestation of the absolute, the operations of the absolute witnessed in the relative, witnessed therefore in and by means of the relative itself—for the human observer is none other that what he observes. As Hegel put it, there is nothing behind the curtain other than that which is in front of it.[3] Or, as Coleridge noted:

> The reality [...] of the objects he has been adoring derives its whole and sole evidence from an obscure sensation which he is alike unable to resist or to comprehend, which compels him to contemplate as without and independent of himself *what yet he could not contemplate at all, were it not a modification of his own being.*[4]

Or Shelley, probing in discussion with Byron the "origin of life":

> We are ourselves the depositories of the evidence we consider.

It is interesting that this witnessing of the divine devolutions, when it occurs in relation to the natural environment, gives a living meaning to the rather abstract pronouncements—whose consequences are difficult to extrapolate—made in some Platonic writings. Just the same applied to the case of the popular notion of pantheism—"everything is God"—which without living experience thereof is rather a thin way, justifiably thought inadequate, of penetrating the meaning of existence. Existence is not known by observing existence, certainly not in the sense that post-Cartesian philosophy has encouraged us in for 250 years. Rather, existence is understood by means of itself. "Life can only be studied in vivo."[5] Again many references could be made to the Indian *advaita* philosophy with which the observations of the European Romantic philosophy so well coincide.[6] It is through the relative that the absolute is comprehended, otherwise it can only remain mere concept, empty of experiential verification. According to the Sufis, only "He who knows himself knows his Lord."[7] This axiom does not imply the unmitigated relativism of modern philosophy, but neither is it the despotic theological dictum of orthodox Christianity or Islam which has, probably more than anything else, been responsible for the decline of those faiths. What the Sufi proverb suggests is that what one knows of Being through one's own experience of being is knowledge of the Reality (*Haqq*)[8] present in the receptacle of relativity. This is what the Taoist mystics meant when they said that "the relative is the absolute," or that "change alone is eternal."[9] It is also significant in this connection that the complexities and voluminous ramifications of Rudolf Steiner's anthroposophy, a system now widespread in the western world, have at their root an initiation exercise which requires contemplative practice in relation to a seed, plant, or flower. Without constant recourse to this basic contemplation, says Steiner, the rest of the entire system will either be incomprehensible, misunderstood, or useless.[10] At the root of German Romantic philosophy, likewise at the root of mystical gnosis in Taoism and Buddhism, is this concern, or direct contact, with the biosphere continuum, what D. H. Lawrence called the Living Principle.[11] It is also probable that the science and discipline of alchemy, with its more or less openly gnostic and spiritual purpose, owed its form to a recognition of the value of understanding organic processes in their *symbolic* function.[12] Thus the contemplative could "come back to Earth" and spare himself the giddiness of the abstract, and at the same time, through witnessing the earth-process, realize his position in relation to soul—its ascent, descent, origin, and destination. William Blake catches this relation between spirit and *physis* in one of the jewel-like epigrams for which he is uniquely famous:

> The Vegetative Universe opens like a flower from the
>   earth's center
> In which is Eternity.[13]

For the mystics and the Romantics, then, the science of symbolism was never, or at most was only incidentally, the science of aesthetically pleasing comparisons between one thing and another. Actually, primarily, it was a science of the real in its various degrees of manifestation.

According to the principles described here from the Cabala and Böhme through to Coleridge and the other Romantics, not to mention the thinkers of our own day who have given attention to this matter, symbol is inextricably related to the Active Imagination and the world to which it is proper, the world of archetypes, *alam-i-arvah* (see chapters 4 and 5). Only thus can the symbol in the German and English Romantics be understood properly. Henry Corbin, who has done so much to open this world to the culture of this half-century, describes the symbol function thus:

> The symbol is not an artificially constructed *sign*: it flowers in the soul spontaneously to announce something that cannot be expressed otherwise; it is the unique expression of the thing symbolized as of a reality that thus becomes transparent to the soul, but which in itself transcends all expression. [...] To penetrate the meaning of symbol is in no sense equivalent to making it superfluous or abolishing

it; for it always remains the sole expression of the signified thing with which it symbolizes. One can never claim to have gone beyond it once and for all, save precisely at the cost of degrading it into allegory, of putting rational, general, abstract equivalents in its place. The exegete should beware lest he thus close himself to the road of the symbol, *which leads out of this world.*[14]

Notice that he implies that the *substrate* of the symbol is the *soul*, which in his work is synonymous with the world of the Active Imagination. So we are emphatically not dealing with the decoding of signs often undertaken in conventional studies of simile, metaphor, or allegory. The symbol is the deed of the symbolic *organ*, which lives in the world of the Active Imagination. That is why the "road of the symbol leads out of this world" into the next one proper to Imagination. Corbin quotes Ahmad Ahsai, a tenth century Persian metaphysician:

The power of imagination is without doubt consubstantial with the soul, it is an organ comparable in that respect to what the hand is for the body.[15]

Now compare Coleridge speaking of Imagination

giv[ing] birth to a system of symbols […] consubstantial with the truths of which they are the conductors.[16]

From the Hindu tradition we read the same:

All the words in books refer fundamentally to data that are derived from physical sense experiences, and if they are to express those far greater aspects of reality that are beyond the level of the senses, it can only be by symbolism that they do so.[17]

There can be no doubt that here we are in the presence of the same matter described by thinkers in widely differing places, times, and cultures. It need hardly be asked whether the impact of such correspondences is strengthened or diminished according to whether Corbin had read Coleridge, or Coleridge had read Ahsai. What does it matter if they are speaking of the same matter?

In the light of the foregoing, one can see what Goethe was aiming to communicate when he said "Look for nothing behind phenomena: they themselves are what is to be learned."[18] The symbols present in the world of nature are, in Corbin's words,

> not so much the object of vision as the organ of vision; what shows the soul, *enables it to see*, the cosmos in which it is and simultaneously what the soul is in this cosmos and what it is in itself.[19]

Symbols, then, "consubstantial with the truths of which they are the conductors" are not restricted to literary technique, strategies of representation, or language. The eye of the soul sees with the energy of that world in which symbols exist: the world of Creative Imagination. Symbols are inherent in life itself. "Alles vergängliche" (the transient, the perishable world) is "Gleichnis" (similitude), according to Goethe's verse.[20] It is the like and the like which symbols express. Thus it is apparent that nature *must* be involved in ontology, the science of being, because its symbols evidence existence speaking to itself of itself. "We are not looking at something other than ourselves on this diagram—we are part of it."[21]

Language—communication—exists on more than one level. In considering existence from the point of view of "sacred grammar" (chapter 2), we see that Böhme, and Coleridge after him, not to mention Blake, pitch divine communication

---

at a level where the "words" of the Sole Existent are the universe itself. This speech of the Ipseity is reflected in the doctrine of Divine Effusion in mystical Islam, Divine Effluence in Böhme's similar image. Next below that come the symbolic utterances of prophets made in verbal sentences but describing experiences in the *barzakh*; and below that again come the discursive proceedings known to us most of the time as "language as such." But that is to see it from the bottom, as it were. Sacred grammar suggests that, viewed from the top, language as such is the Universe as spoken, breathed, sung, effused, by the singular, unpredicable Being. Only in "later" devolutions does language take on the mechanical/logical sequentiality by which it is commonly known to most of us.

It will be clear by now that the poets in whom the esoteric principle is "already sprouting"[22] find that certain verbal symbols are staircases, mediations, as it were, between the levels or worlds of existence, hence the term *barzakh* (bridge, isthmus) in Sufi mysticism. Whereas for practical reasons reference to a sight, sound, or phenomenon of nature or landscape means a pointing by language away from language (toward the "world"), for the contemplative (whose practical reason is not the sole mode of perception), to be referred by linguistic signs to the phenomena of nature is equivalent to being transposed from one level of language to another level of language. The "outer" universe *is* this other level of language: it "expresses," but not as our language-system expects. Here one hears the language of the higher self—Henry Corbin therefore gives the creative imagination, the world where this "upper" language is spoken and comprehended, an alternative name, "creative prayer."[23] According to another writer on mystical poetry,

> Ordinary poets see the beauty of nature, but mystics follow the beauty to the mirror world and seek divine beauty in the archetypes.[24]

This "going beyond," characteristic of the activity of symbolism and of the transposition of levels from profane language to sacred language, Coleridge sees too as the prime function of creative imagination:

> The imagination is the distinguishing characteristic of man as a progressive being.[25]

So it is only in a limited sense of the term *language* that we can correctly say that the phenomena of nature are the symbols most often invoked in contemplative poetry, because they are outside the fabric of language.

Why a limited sense? For on one level it is certainly helpful to think of it in this way, because quite simply when the mouth closes, language stops, and the eye opens on, say, a landscape, rain, or a flower, then there is silence; we are beyond or prior to language, but still in a communion. Wordsworth's famous phrase "an eye made quiet" (in "Lines Written above Tintern Abbey") suggests as one of its several meanings a commingling of the human being as communicative being with the human being as witnessing being. When the eye is really opened, he seems to be saying, it is certain that the tongue is quiet. But when the tongue is quiet, the language of the universe, "voice of silence," is "heard" in the soul world. In this sense it is a limited use of the term *language* when we say language is abandoned in contemplation. From another point of view, contemplation is precisely what translates an already present deeper language, the "grammar of the universe." According to Martin Buber, "in God's response, everything, the universe, is made manifest as language."[26]

In silence is the suggestion and intimation of pure presence, letting go the hold on the categories of space, time, and self. In Far Eastern haiku poetry, as American poets such as Ezra Pound, William Carlos Williams, and Allen Ginsberg were quick to appreciate, phenomena of nature are presented in such immediacy that no discursive or sequential grammar can infuse them at all—this being so to such a point that the verb *to be* is often absent. The same is true of the Hebrew language in which the Divine Name was uttered to Moses; the "am" of the "I am" is a concession made by Western translators of the YHVH, or tetragrammaton. (Is this why Blake transcribed the Hebrew without trying to transliterate or translate it?)[27]

> Languages that omit the verb *be* stress its presence all the more: [...] the tacit link of subject and predicate is even better than the actual verb *be* as a symbol of the lightning flash that locks and illuminates the two poles of an action, creating a phrase. Words are shrunken phrases, compressed riddles. The Word, then, is "Be." All words imply that they *be*, as all realities imply metaphysical experience.[28]
>
> (Elémire Zolla)

It could be said that the more immediate the presentation of a phenomenon in language, the less remote is its next-level symbolic signification; and that the fewer "trappings" it has, the shorter the distance between *mention* and absorption in *the mentioned*. And the hearer of mention, i.e. the reader of a poem or speech, the witness of a natural event, knows the language which mentions, otherwise he cannot hear. Mention, the mentioned, the mentioner, the mentioned to, are the terms in sacred grammar here. The suggestion comes from all directions that they are four modalities of one reality. Neither the dialectical materialist nor the mystic could have occasion to quarrel with this proposition.

If we consider some of the perennial phenomena mentioned in this manner in mystical and Romantic poetry, we will appreciate the degree to which these phenomena, "gestures that speak without the help of language,"[29] reflect ontologically their metaphysical dimensions.

First let us take flowers, for example Wordsworth's daffodils.

> all at once I saw a crowd
> A host of dancing Daffodils
> Along the lake, beneath the Trees
> Ten thousand dancing Daffodils.[30]

Goethe called the perception of the metaphysical principle directly at work in the physical world a primal phenomenon (*Urphänomen*). In agreement with this, Rudolf Steiner's meditation on the archetypal plant was developed.[31] Compare the following descriptions:

> Adepts of the hieratic science take as their starting point the things of appearance and the sympathies they manifest among themselves and with the invisible powers [...] in heaven, terrestrial beings according both to the causal and celestial mode, and on earth heavenly things in a terrestrial state.
>
> What other reason can we give for the fact that the heliotrope follows in its movement the movement of the sun, and the selenotrope[*] the movement of the moon, forming a procession within the limits of their power behind the torches of the universe? Each thing prays according to the rank it occupies in nature, and sings the praise of the divine series to which it belongs, a spiritual or rational or physical or sensuous praise; for the heliotrope moves to the extent that it is free to move, and in its rotation, if we could hear the sound of the air buffeted by its movement, we should be aware that it is a hymn to the king such as it is within the power of a plant to sing. [32]

---

[*]. Selenotropism can be observed in the diurnal leaf movements of the genus *Maranta* (prayer plants) [Author's note]

This was Proclus the Neoplatonist on flowers. Compare Frithjof Schuon:

> The rose differs from the water-lily by its intellectual particularity, by its "way of knowing" and so by its mode of intelligence. Beings possess intelligence in their form to the extent that they are "peripheric" or "passive" and in their essence to the extent that they are "central," "active" and "conscious." [...]
>
> God reveals himself to the plant in the form of the light of the sun. The plant irresistibly turns itself toward the light; it could not be atheistical or impious.[33]

In the ornate style of Kakuzo Okakura the same message is perceived:

> Surely with mankind the appreciation of flowers must have been coeval with the poetry of love. Where better than in a flower, sweet in its unconsciousness, fragrant because of its silence, can we image the unfolding of a virgin soul?[34]

And with this mention of love, following those of *pathos* and *passion*, the hint is given for the hermeneutic circle to close, as the mystic is not only invited but, according to this science of being, required to do. To close the circle, the phenomenon of the flower cannot be considered without the "observer"-participant, the witness, recognizing through sympathy that the "prayer" is his or hers, not only the flower's. Henry Corbin, expanding on Proclus's image of the heliotrope, gives a magnificent exposition of this closing circle, (not to be confused with the "closure" of the poststructuralists, which is more akin to closing off or exhausting a discourse),

an exposition difficult to give in words because of its organic/
experiential locus:

> ... community of essence is perceived in the visible phe-
> nomenon of a flower, in the *tropism* that gives it its name:
> *heliotrope*. But taken as a phenomenon of sympathy, this
> tropism in the plant is at once *action* and *passion*: its action
> (that is to say, its *tropos*, its "conversion") is perceived as
> the action (that is, the attraction) of the Angel or celestial
> prince whose name [helios] for that very reason it bears.
> Its *heliotropism* ... is thus in fact a *heliopathy* (the passion it
> experiences for him). And this passion, this παφοσ is dis-
> closed in a prayer, which is the *act* of this *passion* through
> which the invisible angel draws the flower toward him.
> Accordingly this prayer is the pathos of their *sympatheia*
> and in this [...] is actualized the reciprocal aspiration
> based on the community of essence.

> But since sympathy here is also a condition and mode of
> perception—for it is safe to say that not everyone per-
> ceives this silent prayer offered up by a plant—we must
> also speak of the poetic or cognitive function of sympathy
> in a man like Proclus. As such, it opens up a new dimen-
> sion in beings, the dimension of their invisible selves;
> [...] thus we may speak of a *pathos* experienced by Pro-
> clus in common with the flower, a *pathos* necessary to his
> perception of the *sympathy* which aroused it and which,
> when he perceived it, invested the flower with a
> theophanic function.[35]

Precisely in this disposition of witnessing emerges the role of
the imaginative state in the education of the human being,
which Coleridge and Blake were passionate about, Blake often
to the exclusion, it seems, of any other concern. For Blake the

death of imagination was the death of human possibility itself, perhaps the one great tragedy of human history:

> Reality was forgot, & the Vanities of Time and Space
> Only rememb'red & called Reality.

> How are the Beasts & Birds & Fishes & Plants & Minerals
> Here fix'd into a frozen bulk subject to decay & Death.
> Those visions of Human Life & Shadows of Wisdom &
>   Knowledge
> Are here frozen into unexpansive, deadly destroying
>   Terrors.[36]

That is the world as seen by the materialist, where there is no reciprocity between Earth and spirit because spirit is not acknowledged in the picture, and imagination is given such low status that it appears as if it can do nothing to enter into the world to which it is actually native.

It lies within the potential of the human to "perceive this prayer offered up by the plant," but Corbin admits that not everyone perceives this disposition of the event. What is the difference between the one person and the other? The one who perceives it has entered more lovingly, deeply, into the experience of which he or she is capable than the one who does not. Keats's memorable account of "fellowship with essences" in *Endymion*[37] bears sustained comparison (beyond the eerie similarity of wording) with Corbin's description of the community of essence. Hence it can come as no surprise to hear human perfectibility spoken of as one of the major Romantic themes. But I doubt whether such education in perfectibility as the Romantic writers evoke, and Steiner for instance invites in his gnostic meditations, is understood by all the literary historians to whom the term "perfectibility of man" occurs so easily as a means of getting to grips with a definition of the Romantic movement. But mystics do not compromise: "Perfect man is the most perfect of beings and the very cause of the coming into existence of the world," says Shamsuddin Lahiji.[38]

The very universality—the diversity of sources is large—of this method of developing the human potential should show us that the Romantics did not devise it, but merely reminded us of it at a time when it was much needed, as it continues to be. This sublime philosophy of nature—Perfect Nature here resonates with Perfect Man—returns us again to all the themes covered in the other essays here—the Imagination, the question, the four worlds, the metaphysical conversation, the self, and love. It is no wonder in one sense that the poets of Imagination are almost universally the poets of Nature, too; in another sense it is of course *the* matter for wonder, indeed for a science of wonder. Awe is not fright, but rather an intimation of what we could be waking up to if we made ourselves available. Read in the light of the science of Being, Shelley's *Defence of Poetry* makes total sense as a document of historical, social, psychological, and gnostic knowledge. It cannot be *reduced* to any ideology, as numerous literary critical estimates have done. It can only be raised, if it must be categorized, beyond ideology to the level at which its contents have a function and a possibility of being understood from that level. That event, needful or needless to reiterate, requires a change in level in its witnesses as well as in its protagonists.

With the idea of elevation having become so necessary in this context, it makes sense to proceed from flowers to the next arch-Romantic primal phenomenon which makes its appearance in poetic images of the well-spring, and the mountain which is often its source. The ontological infinite, like the spring, is "self-caused, for something cannot come from nothing any more than a stream can rise higher than its source."[39] So here again we find that what is directly witnessable in the elevation of the mountain, the flow of its stream, and the source as the highest possible mode of its existence, reflects the intellectual principle of the poets and mystics (compare the order of reason, imagination, understanding, and fancy in chapter 4). When Corbin writes:

> The act of being does not take on different meanings, it remains unique, while multiplying itself in the actualities of the beings that it causes to be; an unconditioned Subject which is never itself caused-to-be[40]

he formulates the principle symbolized by the spring in the mountain peak. This correspondence between a physical and a metaphysical principle clarifies for us the unusually high incidence of mountain images in all Romantic poetry, from *The Prelude* to Shelley's "Mont Blanc" to many diaries and notes which confirm, if it needed to be restated, that the fabric of the poetic artifact is intimately bound up with the poets' experiences and self-image, not to mention their immediate physical environment. All these factors, not only the published texts, resound with the metaphysics that were the object of the poets' searches and verbal compositions.

Coleridge, for example, took a minute interest in the phenomenon of the well-spring, noticing more than once the vortex or cone of moving sand, which a spring of otherwise still water produced from its source at the bottom. This image is a curious polar opposite of the high-point or mountain-top which is the location of many such vortices. But for Coleridge as for many a mystical poet or reader animated with the *sympatheia*, it only goes to re-express the ancient Hermetic maxim "As above, so below."[41] The source of the spring produces an inverted mountain as the "devolution" of the water proceeds.[42]

The mountain appears in all the sacred traditions of the world, from the Taoist and Buddhist, the Tibetan Pure Summit,

Mount Kailash,[43] through the Hindu and Muslim (Mount Qaf, the sacred mountain) to the Greek and Christian (Olympus, Mount Athos). The polar relationship of source and summit so precisely imaged in Coleridge's water-cone and its geographical elevation is fundamental to the esoteric tradition. The source is the image and expression of the singular origin to which, if "retrogressed," all extension or ramification would tend, and to the renewal of whose energy all spent forces, in dying, contribute. The spring on the mountain symbolizes the out-flowing of the self-existent non-predicable Ipseity into the "river of life," the descent into multiplicity, the sacred River of Coleridge's "Kubla Khan" which flows to the outmost limits of existentiation, matter, and the material perspective, called in the same poem the "sunless sea." The River of Life does not only flow but descends, physically and metaphysically, from the high point, the source, the tip of the pyramid, which is itself a mountain, whose tip has no dimension because it is the point of their Being—as the Sufis say "without quality,"[44] imaged as non-dimensionality, the "still point of the turning world,"[45] the place where movement, while being originated, is also arrested. The top of the mountain is the image of the fourth world, the *lahut*. The summit is the ultimate expression of unity because it is not only metaphysically but also physically singular. If a peak shares its ground with other peaks, then only the highest will be *the* mountain, the others then become foothills. This is the image of God according to the Quran. "God is and there is not with Him a thing" expresses this ontological priority of the source, the summit.

Such a background also invests the image of the celestial North Pole, about which many interesting observations have been made in literature and in the mystical traditions. The North is mentioned by Indian tradition as *Uttara*,[46] the region of Mount Meru which is identified with the North Pole as early as the Mandeans and Manicheans: "the *terra lucida*, the Earth

---

of light, is situated in the direction of the cosmic North."[47] According to the Sufi mystic Karim al Jili, the earth of the soul is a region in the far north, the only one not to have been affected by the consequences of the fall of Adam. This region's color is green,[48] "its summit touches the lunar sphere," and is inhabited by the mysterious prophet Khidr. Henry Corbin relates this Middle Eastern vision of a paradise in the North to the Western tradition of the castle of the Grail.[49] The North, moreover, expresses the verticality of disposition and vision, the faculty of imagination through which contact with the sacred mountain region is established.[50] The celestial Pole or North Star orients and magnetizes the return and reascent of the pilgrim.

> This word *orient* is interchangeable with North, which is not a horizontal but a vertical pole … the emerald cities and the orient and the North and *Eran-vej* are all on the threshold of a supernatural region where uncreated lights bring into being a shadowless land. It is here that the pilgrim meets his Angel.[51]

Milton mentions the "further North" in *Paradise Lost*, and Blake returns to it many times in his prophetic poems, where Urthona, the Zoa of Creative Imagination, is dedicated to the North.[52] Here, as in the fourfold *mandala* of Tibet and in the Emerald Mountain Qaf of the Sufis, the mountain of mountains is the celestial North, the Heavens, just as the South is the ground, the Earth.[53]

The directional implications of the mountain and the wellspring emerge more actively in the imagery of fire and water, which is amongst the oldest there is, mentioned by the Egyptians and again centrally in the alchemical tradition, where the interaction of heat and moisture are fundamental to the accomplishment of the work. Again because of the relation between verticality and horizontality we can say that fire and water are only other modalities of the totality of which the mountain and descending stream are yet another modality. We are not dealing with different things here, but with different expressions. According to Heracleitus: "this world-order is and shall be ever living fire, kindled in measure and quenched in measure."[54]

Fire is the vertical force, upward, evident in evaporation and heat, eliminating the solidity of matter.[55] Water is the horizontal force, if left to spread it forms the lake (like the well so prominent in the Taoist primeval imagery of the Chinese *I Ching* or Book of Changes), or "ocean." So in their movements or inherent dispositions, fire and water embody the divine contraries of entification (extension, becoming) and annihilation (ascension, passing away), or the in- and out-breathing imaged in the *nafs-er-rahman* (breath of compassion) of the Sufis and given other names by other traditions.[56] In this sense the tests of fire and water undergone by the neophytes in Mozart's *Zauberflöte* represent the test of ability to respond to the fire impulse and the water impulse at the heart of cosmic existence, and therefore at the heart of the human's place of manifestation. For, as we have seen, at every stage the human is no other than that which he contemplates. "Learn, O my friend, that the object of the search is God, and that the subject who seeks is a light that comes from him (or a particle of his light)" says Najm Kubra.[57]

Some of these considerations may go a long way to shedding light on Shelley's profound interest, documented in his life and his published works, in evoking the primal experiences of fire (see chapter 6) and water by deliberate means. They might explain his otherwise anomalous obsession with hot air balloons[58] (illustrating the fire/vertical/flight principle), and his decided penchant for living as close to water as possible (the Thames in England, the Mediterranean in Italy),[59] and that astonishing combination of both interests in his lifelong hobby, building boats out of paper (potentially airborne) and floating them in puddles and streams.

It would not be off the mark to say that Shelley, in such direct evidences of taste for the phenomena just discussed, and Wordsworth and Coleridge on their heroic mountain walks, were all in different ways seeking consciously or unconsciously the invitation which these *Urphänomene* bring about in the potential gnostic, at that stage of readiness that corresponds to Shakespeare's "Ripeness is all." Steiner, following closely the scientific and aesthetic footsteps of Goethe, while at the same time in full comprehension of the mysticism of the East, was in little doubt that the contemplation of nature would make the condition of initiation a reality or felt experience, not the hearsay of legend and superstition.

Shelley, in his *Defence of Poetry*, clearly revealed his strong conviction that these experiences of *sympatheia*, mediated in the world of the Creative Imagination, could afford not only great fulfillment and pleasure to the individual, but could also have limitless social consequences. Poetry, he said, by which he means a type of life which is familiar with the modalities of imaginative vision, and the changes in knowing and being which result from it, could be the new material of "knowledge, power, and pleasure," and could initiate creative action. And it is clear that the knowledge, power, and pleasure experienced in the conditions of extinction of self (see chapters 2, 3, and 8) could only arise out of the extension and experience of compassion, not out of the "anxious need for more security, more gain less loss, and more power over the other."[60]

Perhaps more than any other primal phenomenon, it is the image of birds and flight which has given an idea of the divine human cosmos-relationship. The aspirations of the bird in medieval, renaissance and later poetry and imaginative discourse have everywhere pointed to the fact of "reluctant" incarnation. Whereas fire and water in their principal behavior illustrate one or other of the potentialities at work in an unmitigated form, the *bird* signifies their coexistence in a form which combines incarnation, aspiration, speed, vulnerability, solidity, and insolidity: all marked in the bird's hollow bones—bones being the utmost organic solidification, hence connoting gravity, materiality; and yet a bird's bones, being hollow, deny their own "tendency" and assist the bird's flight. The bird is also adept in three worlds, land, water, and air, and thus able to intimate to human beings seeing the bird with the sympathy of, say, Shelley in his "Skylark Ode" (see chapter 4) that they, too, potentially inhabit three or more worlds. It is in matters like these that the tradition of the winged soul, in which human and bird coexist in the world of archetypes, no doubt originates.[61] Such images well-known to Romanticism as "the viewless wings of Poesy" take on fresh meaning when seen in this light, in that the bird's capability to move from world to world reflects that the knowledge of the archetypal world proper to humankind can be reached on invisible "wings." What is essential is the shifting of level implied, in both the case of the human psychic event or entry into the *alam al mithal* (second world) and the bird's movement from terrestrial space to air. The psychological resonances of the cliché "wing-clipp'd" are also highly suggestive here. The bird is perhaps the one creature whose incarnated state and special possibilities reciprocate and resonate with those hidden in man. This might account for its pride of place in the bestiaries of poetry and myth, whereas some other creatures, for example the tiger, exemplify an energy which, like thunder, is virtually beyond the human's power to emulate.

Blake certainly recognized energy beyond the human, in his poem "The Tyger." For Blake the only possible "fall of humankind" was to fall into blindness and materialism, so that someone under the spell of blindness would not see things in their true light; they would not be seen in their sacred aspect, but only in mean, dull, limited, and finite aspects. He suggested that the energy and power in an animal like the tiger, deemed to be evil, seen another way would be precisely what arouses our sense of wonder, awe, delight, beauty, terror, laughter, mystery. "The howling of wolves, the roaring of tempests," sights like these, he says, are elements of eternity too great for the eyes of humanity to behold as they now are.

The fall of humankind—the evil—if there is one for Blake, lies only in denial of the soul. Body, in the *Marriage of Heaven and Hell*, is not a separate existing principle from soul, as the Cartesian philosophers suggested it was. Body is a portion of soul "let in" by means of the five senses, but not the enemy of soul, not something different from it. This means that the old tradition of hatred of the sense-world and experience in the body wasn't a valid way for Blake, because to deny the body would be an act of soul-amputation, causing injury to the whole system. Long before psychoanalysis came to be defined by Sigmund Freud, Blake had articulated the principle of repression, in his poem "The Poison-Tree," and was to do so again many times, including in the *Marriage of Heaven and Hell*. In denial of the soul lies one of the causes of evil, thinks Blake. Life-energy, if it is refused or manacled, bound up or dammed, will turn poisonous—"Standing water" is Blake's image for this. "Expect poison from standing water." The opposite, flowing water, keeps animals, plants, and whole land-scapes alive. This is why for Blake life is a river, not a puddle of brackish water. Life energy given a channel, in other words, will act creatively, flow will bring about the opposite of poison.

Blake refers implicitly to a science of being whenever he sees in Nature this strange story that bears on the matter of good and evil, and goes much deeper than simply suggesting the positive effects of contemplating scenery. Blake's "magical" background in alchemy and esoteric tradition suggested that nature—if you will, life's raw material—was basically fallen, not in the sense of being morally evil, but in the sense that it was formless and chaotic, like clay, slime, water, dung, mud; not evil as such, just in need of—or capable of receiving—an informant, a kind of ignition or seeding. Blake finds that the raw organic continuum of earth, what he calls "vegetable" or "vegetated" existence, is lent its actuality, character, splendor, by the innumerable varieties of living forms in which it appears, forms which it adopts under the influence of the source which lends it the capacity to transform into the myriad things the universe pours forth. Rarely is nature seen in an absolutely raw state, that is why the apparition of mud, slime, dung, and clay has the air of blindness about it. For Blake, soul, spirit, divine imagination, the upper world of the unfallen, if you like, peoples it, so to speak, with minerals, precious stones, plants, animals, and humans (peopling literally), also with the phenomena of land, sea, sky, weather, light, darkness. Soul sees correctly, according to Blake. Any other eye changes the natural world into a hell, a "frozen bulk […] of deadly destroying Terrors."

Soul here is meant as in the phrase used by Jung, *anima mundi*, world-soul, the factor granting the possibility of uniqueness in everything that lives, not only the human uniqueness which we recognize in the world *character*. In this sense the fallenness of matter in its chaotic raw state is not an irremediable situation, because it is constantly resurrected by the diverse wonders of particular form and its display: form, shape, colour, smell, texture, movement, transformation. That sense of the particular quality is what drives Gerard Hopkins's poems about the living world, and what drives Blake's poem "The Tyger." It is a metaphysical poem, not really a nature poem, because it sees in the Tyger the expression of a quality unique to that animal. The Tyger is *informed* matter; the rabbit is very differently informed matter; the chicken very differently again. Blake often muses on this mysterious quiddity, thisness, of various living forms.

———

The rat, the mouse, the fox, the rabbit watch the roots;
the lion, the tyger, the horse, and the elephant watch the
fruits.

> Does the Eagle know what is in the pit?
> Or will thou go ask the mole?
> Can wisdom be put in a silver road
> Or love in a Golden Bowl?

With what sense is it that the chicken shuns the raven-
  ous hawk?
With what sense does the tame pigeon measure out the
  expanse?
With what sense does the bee form cells? have not the
  mouse and frog
Eyes and ears and sense of touch? yet are their habita-
  tions
And their pursuits as different as their form and as their
  joys.
Ask the wild ass why he refuses burdens, and the meek
  camel
 Why he loves man: is it because of eye, ear, mouth, or
  skin,
Or breathing nostrils? No, for these the wolf and tyger
  have.
Ask the blind worm the secrets of the grave, and why
  her spires
Love to curl round the bones of death; and ask the
  rav'nous snake
Where she gets poison, & the wing'd eagle why he loves
  the sun;
And then tell me the thoughts of man, that have been
  hid of old.[62]

The way Blake sees things is so deeply rooted in esoteric per-spectives that it can appear strange to the everyday eye. We are made to feel the rawness of the material of nature, its "vegeta-ble mass," at the same moment as we are called to behold the splendor of the various determinations it has had conferred on it, seeded in it, by the upper heavens. The idea of *tiger* drifting down into DNA, into that organic material with the capacity to produce form but not yet having produced it; the genetic blue-print of *tiger* initiating the gradual incidence of form from the formless—from a blob of mucus into a tiger. Blake in his ram-bling discourses on the fallenness of base matter asks us to see this matter, *prima materia*, simultaneously with the splendor of the creature, and *to realize our life as this*, to realize these con-trary aspects as one. This was not usual for Blake's time, and it still isn't very usual for ours. The spiritual power of this vision along with its intimacy with physical life is beautifully captured by Llewellyn Vaughan-Lee when he says "Our reflective powers not only separate us from the animal world; they also allow us to look into the depths of the unconscious without being assim-ilated back into that primal world."[63]

The Indian poets and philosophers used essentially the same idea as Blake's, in the traditional symbol of the lotus-flower, occurring so often in their writings and so oddly to Western eyes. The roots of the lotus are anchored in thick, colorless, muddy water; the flower rises out of it in perfect clarity, form; luminescent colour. The miracle is in the perfection of form in so obvious an intimacy with such muck. Its expression of the contraries is complete in this way, like Blake's images of nature. Blake always drops the same kinds of hint, which might be expanded in some such way as to say that the miraculous always comes of a mergence between the clean and the unclean, Heaven and Hell, good and evil. The gardener who knows that strong dung makes for good flowers is not making a moral judgement, though a perception exists there about the perfection of life and the conditions that make it come about. This is a very difficult thing to explain, but it is at the root of Blake's outraged tough protests and his satirical outbursts about conventional views of good and evil, views that were given political sanction by the church and state.

Two more strange things. One is that "the seeds of contemplative thought," as Blake calls them, the ideas (*logoi spermatikoi*) that inform matter and raise it from the fallen state, are said in his esoteric tradition to be so strong that they exist independently of any specific example of them.

> [The] world of Imagination is Infinite and Eternal, whereas the world of Generation, or Vegetation, is finite & temporal. There Exist in that Eternal World the permanent Realities of Every Thing which we see reflected in this Vegetable Glass of Nature. All things are comprehended in their Eternal forms in the divine body of the Saviour, the true Vine of Eternity, the Human Imagination. [...]

> The eternal nature & permanence of [Imagination's] ever-existent Images is considered as less permanent than the things of Vegetated & Generated Nature; yet the Oak dies as well as the Lettuce, but its eternal image & Individuality never dies, but renews by its seed; just so the Imaginative image returns by the seed of Contemplative Thought.
>
> (Blake, *Last Judgement*, § 1)

Species exist in this way, not totally dependent on any one instance of the species. The species called *tiger* entered into Blake's knowledge without his ever having seen a tiger alive. Probably not even a stuffed one. Seeing a painting was probably the only contact he had with the reality of tigers other than hearsay, most of that probably not accurate. Such is the precision and feel, as well as passion, with which Blake has intuited his tiger, that he drops the hint that *anima mundi*, soul of the world, can inform even where the actual animal can't be seen. Blake would have found no difficulty accepting this.

The other is a proverbial phrase in the writings of the alchemists which Blake studied. It is well known that the alchemists expressed themselves as being in quest—in rather the same manner as knights in quest of the holy Grail—of what they referred to as the philosopher's stone. Notoriously enigmatic in defining what this was, they nevertheless committed themselves to remarks such as: If you know where to look, the philosopher's stone is as easy to find as a piece of dirt, it comes from the lowest of the low. And yet the reason for its being sought after is that it can turn anything it touches into gold.

The common world, seen with the eye of soul, is the key to metaphysical mysteries. Blake has never been seen as "nature poet," and indeed he consciously contrasted himself with Wordsworth, saying that mere descriptions of natural objects did little for him but "stifle and deaden the imagination in me." But at the alchemical level, what we might call the level of the science of Being as seen in symbol, it is clear that Blake saw Nature with the eye of pure Light, offering not descriptions but intuitions. "If the doors of perception were cleansed, everything would appear as it is, Infinite."

The outer world, then, when read as a "book of nature" with the eye of similitude and the energy of soul (imaginative sight, initiated by the pure light, causeless cause of seeing), offers a datum, a communication, not different from the inner world of humankind but in consonance with it. For while the external world of nature (the first of the four worlds) must remain limited if seen with the eyes of the first world, it is, if seen through the eye of light—the eye of the *mithal*—instinct with the higher causes and consonant with them as their words, deeds, and forms. The I AM, Coleridge said, has as its "choral echo" nothing other than this universe.

8

FEDELE D'AMORE

The Essence and Arts of Love

Today, like every other day
We awake empty and scared.
Do not enclose yourself in a book.
Open your voice and sing.
Let the beauty we love be what we do.
There are hundreds of ways to kneel and kiss the ground.
—RUMI

Only in virtue of his power to enter into relation is man
able to live in the spirit.
—MARTIN BUBER

Beauty is truth, truth beauty,—that is all
Ye know on earth, and all ye need to know.
—Keats, "Ode on a Grecian Urn"

BEAUTY IS KNOWN AS THE OBJECT of inclination, the object of
love, to most of us most of the time. Keats's world-renowned
choice of words implies that it is also the object of a *knowing*
inclination. Beauty is truth, he says, and the nature of truth is
that it can be contacted only by a knower. And the only true
knower, according to the mystical and esoteric traditions, is a
lover by virtue of his knowing, and a knower by virtue of his
loving.

Keats's two lines make a statement in poetry that can all too
easily be deadened by repetition. Let us rethink this truthful
inclination to beauty. Why did Keats find it so compelling as to
end his "Ode on a Grecian Urn" with this thought? The meaning

of the couplet might be illuminated by comparing what happens to iron under the influence of a magnetic field. The piece of iron, or the compass needle, aligns itself in a motion which is at once fluid and exact. Fluid, in that there is the swing and pull of the material in relationship to gravity, there is some momentum. Exact, in that the direction of alignment is certain. In the case of the compass, to North and South; in the case of magnetizable metal, simply the nearest field of magnetism.

All we know on Earth, says Keats, is that Beauty is the source according to which Knowers incline in their love of truth; the source according to which their inner compass is aligned.

But there is more. Why does Keats add "all we need to know"? If we know it, as he says we do, why do we also "need to know" it? Two seeming opposites: we know something, and need to know it.

A piece of iron will align itself to the influence of a magnetic field. This is because it "knows." The human being is like this, says Keats, because the human knows Beauty when it appears: "All we know on earth."

> It is a simple recognition of the natural and presumably biological law that whatever is perceived as reality emits a compelling fascination indistinguishable from beauty,[1]

says Ted Hughes, referring to the poet's relationship with the Great Goddess of Complete Being, the Muse, "the wholly beautiful," whom the poet will worship "though it slay [him]."

The iron responds to the magnet. It knows. But something more can happen to it. It can itself become magnetized, so that it can align itself to the earth's magnetic field and be changed from a passive respondent to magnetism into a compass. In this magnetized state it can cause other iron objects to incline to itself. It had a knowledge, which was to respond to magnetism; and had also a need, to become a

---

magnet itself, so that it might attract toward it what it itself once was.

Its possibility extends further still, to turning into a magnet what it first only attracted. This is the third stage of the knowledge of Beauty. It is catching.

If we know the beautiful when we see it, we can say we realize what Keats means by "all we know on earth." If then we wish to become beautiful ourselves, if we wish to become magnetized by the beauty we acknowledge, then we not only know, but also need to know. This is where the paradox finds its solution. To respond to beauty is one stage, to be magnetized by it is another.

So Keats's oft-quoted phrase, along with all its Neoplatonic forerunners, means much more that it seems to mean when it trips off the tongue or is trotted out in hackneyed (whether or not literary) contexts. It means that *knowing is itself an invitation to a response*. There is, in short, not only something to be recognized, but something to come of it. The piece of iron not only knows, but needs to know. It responds to magnetism, and needs to become a magnet. And love is just as near a description of this magnetism as is knowledge. Here again we are living in more than one world.

Love is the action by which inclination toward Beauty happens. Beauty is the source, Love is the action which returns knowledge, by the fact of its inclination, to its source. So for Keats, as his couplet indicates to us, *knowing* is not separated off, in the head, from a *love* drowned somewhere in emotions. Keats reminds a jaded imagination that love and knowledge are not the adversaries that our culture sometimes tries to call them. Rather, they are the two root words of the word *philosophy* [*philo* = love, *sophia* = knowledge]. And this, if you wish to put it like this, is where the trail of Eros (love) and Psyche (soul) begins. Sophia is a woman's name because knowledge was once felt to be the presence of the female. The Great Goddess, Isis,

Sophia, and the woman called Philosophy in Boethius's vision (and Chaucer's rendering of it), are one and the same.

This knowledge, approached in the light of Keats's conundrum, is a much richer affair than what mostly passes for knowledge, the quiz-consciousness of retention and regurgitation, storage and retrieval, and the discursive agility prized by academics and academic philosophers. This different, gnostic, direct knowledge is knowledge of the origin of the human situation, and particularly a taste of its meaning and its quality. It is not a quantitative enumeration of its structure.

Taste and the sense of tasting were important to Keats for just this reason. Taste is a reminder that knowledge by taste is a more direct affair than knowledge by the head alone. From this fact originates Keats's celebrated emphasis on the tasting of fruits, a celebration of the mouth particularly, in eating, drinking, kissing, and erotic play. He defies the prudish, and annoyed the critics of his day, by constant reference to intimate sexual contact. And in such intimacy he imaged one location—the prime matter of creation at the level of alchemical water, the "moist soul"—in which the future has the potential to actualize itself.

He was also familiar with the melancholy of the discarnate spirit who enters into matter by these very means. Normally, spiritual beauty attracts upwards, physical beauty downwards, and the attractions may be felt coming from the same source when a human being inclines toward another because of beauty, whether interior beauty, exterior beauty, or both. There may be melancholy in the incarnate entity who wishes to depart from matter, just as there is desire in the discarnate spirit which is drawn to enter it, and lovers are subject to the message coming from both directions. Does this ambiguity perhaps occupy the fact that, while one of the deepest if not the deepest of human experiences, love is often felt to be one of the most mixed? Did Keats, like Blake's pre-incarnate Thel, remember Heracleitus: "It is delight or death to souls to become moist. It is delight to them to fall into birth." And of souls in relation to incarnated beings, Heracleitus adds: "We live their death[,] they live ours."

Perhaps Keats's ode may not seem at first sight to be a quintessential love poem. But nor are Rumi's poems standard love poetry addressed by human partner to human partner only. Such writing as Keats's ode and Rumi's poetry, being grounded in love, springs directly from it. The Romantics, though always capable of writing conventional love poems, nevertheless had a special claim to the very contact with love that the creative spirit of poetry itself could be said to have. The special quality of Romantic poetry is its ability to imply a fundamental affinity between love and the poetic principle, and the principle of creativity. Like Rumi's work, the poetry of the Romantics lives on the deeply held axiom that love lies at—at the deepest level *is*—the root of existence itself.

Toward the end of such a study of creativity as we have conducted in the other essays, it should be clear that neither a psychology of love, nor a sociology or history of love, nor a theology of love, nor a bestiary of love, is in place here; in what we have suggested as a *gnosiology* of Romanticism the categories just named, though comprehended, can have only a limited and limiting force. They cannot be applied alone to the aims and the matter of the Romantic poets, nor to their contemplative and metaphysical forebears.

That love means different things to different people may be a banal truth, but where principles of interpreting human behavior and culture are concerned, the banality fades and the relevance deepens. All consideration of love proceeding from human specialisms such as psychology, history, sociology, politics, economics, are finite, and they end, in some sense, before a consideration of the poets can even begin. In a gnosiology, on the other hand, we are constantly inviting a face to

face encounter with that which grants the possibility of any categories arising at all. Not with the data, but with the donor,
"the Presence," says Henry Corbin,

> whose supra-being consists in *causing-to-be*, and which for
> that reason can never itself be *caused-to-be*, nor seen as
> being—forever invisible while *causing-to-see* in its perma-
> nent actuation of each act of being.[2]

So when asking a gnosiological question about love-poetry, we
come to a perspective which might speak of love being the
source of perception, instead of love being viewed under the lens
of a particular mode of thought or enquiry.

We could say that in the foregoing chapters, all the expectations that we and the humanistic culture in general normally
hold of what the self is, what time is, what language can and
cannot do, what asking questions means—all these expectations are the first things which a gnosis or gnosiology does away
with, abandons, renders extinct, or simply cannot address
because they exist at the "wrong level." To say this is not the
same as existential nihilism, because that ideological position
still maintains some sort of hold on a self "tragically" lost. In
nihilism "we can be disillusioned in this way but in ourselves
remain unchanged: through our personality we can be just as
dependent upon the opinion of other people as before, and we
can remain subject to negative states, though we know that the
world in which our personality lives can give us nothing."[3] In
the experience which is the subject of a gnosiology, in the experience which I suggest was the aim and destination of the
Romantics' speculative and creative work, there is literally no
personality left to tend the embers of nihilistic or pessimistic
thought patterns, and no reliance can be placed on the powers
of analysis the philosophers have devised. Here, literally, "no
metaphor can convey [...] that you did not throw when you

threw."[4] A gnosiology such as the one we have attempted to enter into in the last seven chapters regarding the human being as the place, the locus, of an action, not as the origin, doer, agent, has no place for nihilism. Therefore oriental mysticism, which is gnosiology in a traditional, practical framework of expression, subsists without the notion of self or personality— that notion does not have to be wiped out, it is a sense already not there in the first place.[5] So here too, there is no talk of nihilism. The mystics' stricter point of view, the apogee of their logic, suggests that it is out of place to see anything there as needing to be annihilated. Here again the very extremity of what is being said only bears witness to the equal and opposite force with which our culture entrenches the notion of self as an inalienable stronghold, bearer of rights. "Ego says I am here. Egotism says I am right,"[6] remarked David Bohm. And where love, like self, is concerned, this polarization of misunderstandings can be astronomical, to the point at which the word *love*, used at the different poles, can mean its own opposite, and threaten to close down its possibilities of indication completely.

One basic means of coming to an understanding of the poetic principle and its affinity with love is to recall the analogies offered by the "sacred grammar," but this time as revealed in the difference between active and passive in language. For whereas language in one mode, the discursive, denies the eventuation of awareness in dimensions outside the range of discourse, in another mode, what we call sacred grammar, it reveals the metaphysical principles often forgotten by the practitioners of the discursive mode in all its "enlightened" reasonableness.

So, where love is concerned, sacred grammar prepares and proposes the existence of the lover, the loved, and the love itself. Translated, it reads *active*, *passive*, and *reconciling*.[7] The gerund, *ing*, is the mark of creativity in its existentiating mode, creating duration, existence, entification, manifestation, that which is "in a business," in a process, what we have called elsewhere a devolution. This devolution or business is the knowing inclination of which Keats speaks, by which beauty is known to be truth.

Alongside this indication, the grammar of the universe also proposes that in the singularity of the verb *to be* is sometimes hinted, or sometimes revealed that, in essence, existence is a unity; and that the principal order of derivation is from the one to the many (manifestation), even though the temporal order observed at some moments may be perceived as the contrary. In fact language, in principles like "active" and "passive," nearly always hypostatises a process that in any given situation and instance is hardly ever complete. The dying can witness the living, just as the living can witness the dying; in other words, in manifestation these principles of the sacred grammar are "dissolved" i.e., *in solution*, relativised, rather than absolute as they are in principial cognition, which is the cognition, by the first principle, of itself.[8]

So when we speak of the verb *to be*, or of *is*ness, we also imply the singularity of being. But when we distinguish active from passive, we are on a level of distinctions, where the multiplicity starts.

If existence is a unity, then existence's devolution and multiplicities must be the same, and yet from another point of view, different. Here we are on the threshold of a metaphysics of gnosis[9] (not to be exclusively identified with Manichaean gnosticism) which in all traditions speaks of the self-manifestation of the singular existent, Sole Being: this in Taoist, Hindu, Buddhist, Sufi, Hermetic, and theosophical traditions alike.[10]

This singular existent is the principle or metaphysical root of the divine conversation described in an earlier chapter. The fact that Coleridge was discovering in landscape a forgotten "truth of his own inner nature" was an intimation of the "essential" identity of knower and known, self and world, lover

155

and loved: an ontological identity which conditioning does so much so early to cover and conceal that we come to feel, as the Rationalists and materialists did, that it is not a fact.[11] Gnostic metaphysics, as much as Keats's equation of love and knowledge, is a statement that it is a fact, insofar as it is possible to state such a fact without gnostic experience, in which alone the realization of an essence can take place. If there is only one existence, ultimately, then the only real realization can be realized only by that existence; there can be no other realizer. This is what is referred to in the Indian *advaita* tradition by the statement that the only object of consciousness is consciousness itself, just as the only agent of consciousness is consciousness itself. In other words, contrary to the Western dualist assumption, the world is consciousness in its objective aspect, and consciousness is matter in its subjective aspect.

In the phenomenon of metaphysical conversation discussed in chapter 3 we find that the essential identity of knower and known is imaged in terms of a conversation, a situation in which it is assumed that both participants are like beings and know the language they are using. It explains why the transition from the image of a conversation between human beings to the image of a conversation between a human being and the natural world or landscape, seems so effortless, and yet from the existentialist-rationalist position so unreasonable. For in the world of essence, unacknowledged by the *ratio*, self and world are in "intimate dialogue," as are all evidences of polarity in nature, wherever the distinction between speaker and hearer, actor and patient, giver and receiver, lover and loved, occurs. At any and every moment the relative roles change, of course, but the polarity exists because intimacy is a metaphysical (as well as physical) necessity of self-manifestation if the sole being is to actualize, to become an event out of a latency. Is a gnosiology of love-poetry, then, necessarily a metaphysics of affinity, intimacy? I think it is.

―――――

We find ourselves here pointed toward a level quite out of the ordinary. We find that the mystics and metaphysicians speak of themselves as lovers, *fedeli d'amore*, and of their process as the path of love, or the way of the heart, or the way of compassion. The poets like Coleridge speak of the universe existentiating in *adoration* of the I AM, the Ipseity, and freely invoke the Apocryphal incarnation of Wisdom as She, the Creative feminine: "the breath of the power of God." Given the severity of their discipline and the extent of their intellectual achievements, the originators of these formulations cannot be reproached with bearing a trace of the sentimentalizing which has made love "mentioned by its name" such an outcast in twentieth century poetry and fiction. Perhaps it is a clarification to say that the danger of sentimentalizing disappears along with the arch-sentimentalizer, which is the ego or self. For in the gnostic experience there is no other self but the self of the unique, and its sentiment is beyond anything we could have the capacity, let alone the right, to castigate or criticize. And since we actually are the resultant of the sentiment of the unique toward its own qualities we can as well disown that sentiment as destroy ourselves entirely. The nuclear eventuality has for us become the fulcrum, therefore, between the ego of passion and the self of compassion. Much is implied in the difference between passion and compassion, in that the fundamental attraction and yearning [*passion*] is present in both but in *com*passion it is the *mutual* attraction of the individual soul and its originary ground, a *sympatheia*,[12] which seeks a meeting and not a possession.

We find then that the language of affinity, intimacy, love, is natural to metaphysics quite as much as it is to the world of poetry and to the physical attraction between sexes or to the affinity of friendship. And the fact that such language is applicable at all at these different levels must suggest that ultimately they are not to be divided without misunderstanding, loss, or at the very least, the failure of a certain potential to realize itself in a certain situation.

Philip Sherrard's statement "When I say 'I love', I am really misappropriating something that is not mine, but which is expressing itself through me"[13] is an example of the perspective of a lover whose identity has undergone—as it were in a crucible—the experience of gnosis or transformation. From one point of view it is a recognition of a priority, of the relation between the necessary and the contingent: the same relation as subsists between the active and passive, though always in constant movement. Without wishing to theologize a discussion which the poets and metaphysicians "of the Heart" insist is beyond the names of different faiths,[14] the same priority is apparent in St. Paul's phrase "not I, but Christ in me." This is as radical a shift in perspective for the non-gnostic state as is the Buddhist proposition that what you think of as your self is nothing at all, at most, simply an accretion of conditionings.[15] The priority devolves, as it does in the sacred grammar, on who is permitted to use the word "I."[16] The purest of the traditions of mystical gnosis, rather like the Hebrews who prohibited the saying of the tetragrammatic YHVH, forbid use of the first person, because any contingent being using it takes on the role of usurper in so doing.[17]

I'm a predicating creature in some ways. It's a question of which way the attention is. If I […] predicate "I AM," then my attention is the wrong way. But the "I AM" will be predicated through me. It means I'm creating, there's nothing I can do to stop creating sub-wholes, and that is OK as long as my identification isn't in those sub-wholes. I have a responsibility for them, for the things I make manifest. But the I AM is not something I am trying to predicate. It will be predicated through me, and that then becomes my friend, my home. […] The way I think and act, in some way is meaning, and I will either be at a coarse or a subtle level, depending on my relationship with the I AM. [...] As long as I accept that, I am going to create sub-wholes, but I don't want to treat that as me.[18]

So someone saying "I love" without awareness is, unless making the allowance described by the quoted speaker, "liable to regard [love] as little more than an expression of his own ego, to use or abuse as he thinks fit."[19] So it may be clearer now than it was before that an effective interpretation of the Romantic poets' concern with love depends unconditionally on the tact with which it is raised, a tact which must acknowledge who we are and who we think we are,[20] before we can come to the question of *who loves* in the love relationship.

This tact is one which our present culture's views of self, civilization, and humanity's *raison d'être* makes it nigh-on impossible to observe. But the way in which love enters into the reflections of the poets affords the reader a possibility of insight into it.

Loss of this tact, or suspension of the ability to practice it, is the very *dejection* of which Coleridge's ode speaks so directly. It is a dejection related profoundly to the lack of love toward which a false perception of personality must inevitably tend. Coleridge expressly mentions

> that inanimate cold world allowed
> to the poor loveless ever-anxious crowd,

and refers to what has often puzzled critics,

> a fair luminous cloud
> Enveloping the earth—

a cloud which is the veritable transformer of lovelessness to love, cold to warmth, anxiety to peace, the inanimate to the

animate; from death to life, in fact. Coleridge states it as a con-
ditional clause:

> *would we* aught behold of higher worth,
> than that inanimate cold world allow'd
> to the poor loveless ever-anxious crowd,
>   Ah! from the soul itself must issue forth
> A light, a glory, a fair luminous cloud
>   Enveloping the earth—
> And from the soul itself must there be sent
>   A sweet and potent voice, of its own birth
> Of all sweet sounds the life and element![21]

"Of its own birth … the life and element" gives us the necessary
hint that the soul from which this cloud may issue is not equivalent to the empirical self or personality but rather an expression from the *world of soul.* The empirical self's world is
inanimate matter, and Coleridge's hint here is that because that
self only allows a cold world, an inanimate world, it is "loveless,"
cut off from love: it has failed to recognize its own true existence in the source of love, the soul which meets with its own
when the world is warm, animate, love-filled. The soul, says Coleridge, sends out the voice of its own birth and in this way the
earth is animated. We are reminded of Böhme: "Everything has
its mouth to manifestation: this is the language of nature."[22]
We are animate: we *are* nature, not simply observers of
nature.[23] The moment the dualist-separatist consciousness
enters in, the world turns cold, inanimate, and the self turns
out to be at once anxious in acquisitiveness and poor in
achievement. The metaphysically significant affinity, on the
other hand, is vehicled by love; it is an acknowledgment
between lovers of "whose love it is that validated their lives."[24]
Such is perhaps the "paradisal state" or even the example of
perfectible humanity. And, like Coleridge's verse that indicates

simultaneously the potential and the lack of humanity's relationship with nature, Philip Sherrard suggests "it is some such
failure of acknowledgment that results in the fall from the
paradisal state of which the change in consciousness from the
sacred to the profane is both the cause and symptom."[25]

We know from an earlier version that Coleridge's ode was
written under the direct pressure of an intimate relationship,
in the form of a letter.[26] In its finished form it is no less intimate, but its augmented capacity as a statement at once intimate and metaphysical is made quite plain. The provenance
of this type of statement bears more than a passing resem-
blance to that of the writings of some mystics (for example Ibn
'Arabi's love poetry),[27] which is the direct result and illustra-
tion of intimacy both in the human world and in the worlds of
imagination and beyond. The peculiar power of such docu-
ments is their suggestion that that "far off" place is what the
intimacy of the here and now is totally dependent on, related
as the contingent to the necessary. This intimacy in itself is
sometimes sufficient, then, to accomplish the annihilation of
ego-states which the metaphysicians, ascetics, and monastics
sought by avoiding company and sexual love. But the very
example of the mystical love poems reinforces our need to
acknowledge that these borderlines between isolation and
involvement are far from hard and fast.

As was said in an earlier chapter, the conjunction of the love-
poem and the esoteric process of self-extinction as practised in
all the traditions of the world demonstrates, as Coleridge's
verse does, that love is not only the best thing in existence but
the very *allower* of existence. The living world is "allowed" by
love just as only an "inanimate cold world" is "allowed" by the
loveless. Whereas Coleridge's "Dejection Ode" speaks of the
necessity of love through its lack, Keats affirms it: "I am con-
vinced of only this: the holiness of the heart's affections and
the truth of imagination." His "vale of soul-making," though a

metaphysically precise image, implies also a laboratory for soul-education whose main source of energy is "imagination, and the heart's affections."[28] Metaphysical power is here vehicled by love, as it is in the mystics' discourses. The empirical self, the "individual" vaunted by the cultists of the so-called Romanticism, is not the source of love but the *locus* of love; just as—when it likewise uses "I" to speak of its experiences—it is not telling the truth about its real contingency to the Singular Being which first grants the possibility of speech. This is a profound difference on which rest many far-reaching consequences in the world of our common awareness, as well as our scientific and philosophical investigations. The individual not being seen as the source of love, only one avenue is left to the gnostic—like Blake, he must in the end realize that love is the source of the individual. "Every natural Effect has a Spiritual Cause."

So, just as in traditional metaphysics the universe and life are the outflown breath, word, speech of the singular Ipseity, likewise the human, the microcosmic entity, speaks potentially the "luminous cloud," which is its possible instancing or reflection of the love which its form is intended to express. There are of course levels on which love is spoken as well as acted, and the poetry of love, just like the metaphysics of love, is one of them.

When the seeker has been found he looks through the eyes of his child and sees the secrets of his own heart.[29]

(Vaughan-Lee)

And we are put on earth a little space
That we may learn to bear the beams of love.[30]

(Blake)

When God sympathizes with one of his servants, this means He causes compassion to exist in him, that is through him, so that he becomes capable of sympathizing with other creatures. God does not take him as an object of compassion, but invests him with this divine attribute, whereby he experiences compassion for others.[31]

(Corbin)

Passages like these simultaneously concentrate and present the levels and meanings of love from the point of view which we have attempted to suggest in the first part of this chapter. We are presented with the love of parent to child ("He looks through the eyes of his child"), lover to beloved, master to servant, and necessary to contingent ("bear the beams of love"). We are invited to view the principial similarity of all the pairings: need–response, passion–compassion, pathetic–sympathetic, question–answer, departure–return. They could be described as polarized affinities in the process of, or on the point of, coming together.[32] Indeed the very notion of affinity holds within itself the mystery of "the one and the many" which Coleridge pondered so constantly, for it implies a kind of duality which is nevertheless anything but an estrangement. Or, it implies unity which contains in itself a wish for reflection (bending-back), an *act* of becoming conscious. As Jung put it, reflection is "an act whereby we stop, call something to mind, form a picture, take up a relation to and come to terms with what we have seen."[33]

According to Indian tradition, consciousness is identical with the Divine or Sole Existence,[34] and at the same time the human being is specially empowered to perform the act of reflection—for most purposes this faculty distinguishes us from other forms of animal and vegetable life, and from inanimate life (although from the esoteric point of view it is all a matter of degree, for, having come to an especially high position *vis-à-vis* the environment, we must therefore have comprehended or passed through the other stages of life—and hence the other stages can be said to be none other than, but not, human. Rumi writes:

> I died as mineral and became a plant, I died as plant and rose to animal, I died as animal and I was man.[35]

(Mathnawi, Book 3)

The fact, then, that the Ground of Being is Divine Consciousness, coupled with our disposition for reflection, explains the traditional saying that we are made in God's image. Thus we arrive, through logic, at a consideration of priorities which used to be constated through faiths, dogmas, theologies.[36] The reason it is important to raise the matter here is not to prove or to disprove a theological postulate but to gain insight into the paradoxical mixture, as celebrated as it is misunderstood, of the love impulse in mystical poetry and the mystical impulse in love poetry.

When Blake says our existence comes about in order "to learn to bear the beams of love," he is expressing exactly the tradition we have considered, namely that the learning concerned is precisely of the fact that we are not the agents but the patients, not the originators but the bearers, of an energy which itself is the sole spoken word of the strictly First Person Singular, the Divine I.[37] Depending, then, on the level from which these "beams" are witnessed, or at which they are carried, they will either seem to come from elsewhere, (perhaps from a person) or from nowhere: "out of the blue," "like much needed rain," "like a windfall"—it is interesting how the traditional images which remain in clichés always have their metaphysical meanings almost intact: "wind" is the spirit, "rain" is mercy, "the blue" is the heavens. It all depends on the level of the witness, or on the state of the witness, how this love will be manifest: a child will witness the love (or lack of it) of the parent without

knowing its name or consciously comparing it with other manifestations. As Blake said, vision, and what is seen, depends on
the "eye that beholds it," "as perceptive organs vary, so objects
seem to vary." This is reflected also in the ninety-six names for
love in the Sanskrit language.[38]

When Coleridge reflects in his "Dejection Ode" on the "fair
luminous cloud enveloping the earth" so urgently necessary
for the abatement of dejection, he is speaking of the light—
the Christ-light: "I am the light of the world"[39]—in whose
beams Blake says we live in order to learn to mediate (not
dominate); this cloud is, as it were, the world of love to which
we owe all being, all consciousness, all possibility of growing,
reproducing, dying; an energy which vehicles all the four
"worlds" described in chapter 5.

The Romantic poets speak of this love as being present in and
invited by the wonders of nature. This prefigures the extraordi-
narily fertile analogies that esoteric metaphysics finds in the
fields of ecology and the post-Newtonian sciences, which offer
our conditioned and suspicious mentalities a rest from the outworn connotations and sentimentalizing of the hackneyed
imagery of love poetry, and invite perhaps a cooler contemplation of the reality of the oneness of Being and the interdependence, down to the most infinitesimal degree, of all life forms.
But when the murkier emotions connoted by some forms of
spiritualism and religious belief (and their associated morbid
or tyrannical outcomes) are strained off, or allowed to sink to
the bottom as it were, then ecology and the new physics suggest
very real affinities with the mystical love poetry of the esoteric
metaphysicians and the Romantic poets. Compare Coleridge's
exclamation

Ah, Lady! we receive but what we give[40]

with the Buddhist

> We are what we think.
> All that we are arises with our thoughts.
> With our thoughts we make the world.[41]

and the modern thinker Kühlewind's remark:

> naive realism—the deeply rooted attitude that there exist
> perceptions, thoughts, facts and so forth *without my partici-*
> *pation*—that all these are simply "there" is [...] difficult to
> overcome.[42]

Jung suggested thought—reflection—was a higher function
in humans because it works in "contradistinction to the com-
pulsion of natural law."[43] From this position it is easy to take
the next step, which is to say that the thought world, the Light
of Consciousness, is a higher law, a world in which we live all
the time, although our civilization has so firmly shut the door
on this higher world that the first world becomes "cold,"
"inanimate," "anxious," and "loveless"; and no wonder.

The fair luminous cloud, the *rigpa* of the Tibetans,[44] appears
in this world as a diaphaneity, as an infusion. All the "worlds"
infuse or interfuse in one another, as Wordsworth's choice of
words in his poem "Tintern Abbey" so carefully tried to indicate:

> And I have felt
> A presence that disturbs me with the joy
> Of elevated thoughts; a sense sublime
> Of something far more deeply interfused,
> Whose dwelling is the light of setting suns,
> And the round ocean, and the living air,
> And the blue sky, and in the mind of man,
> A motion and a spirit, that impels
> All thinking things, all objects of all thought,
> And rolls through all things.[45]

———

The infusion, if we consent to its constant invitations, allows the love-affair, on whatever level it is conducted, to take place. Infusion is a very important image in these studies because it goes further than the simple image of immersion, itself often used in mystical poetry. Infusion, unlike immersion, changes the nature of the entities which meet in infusion. Hence the tremendous depth of significance to be apprehended in all cooking processes, and in the oriental tea ceremony,[46] a thing so much forgotten in our twentieth century "humanistic" culture that tea-parties have become one of the images of triviality, not depth. Alas for our tired imagination that the alchemy of nature is no longer infusing culture as it so easily, effortlessly, could. For the effort is not really ours, it is the disposition of being itself to occupy these states as it is the disposition of a rose to bloom or a snail to make a shell. No one knew as well as Rumi the extent of the power of love. The cook says to the pea:

> Don't try to jump out.
> You think I'm torturing you.
> I'm giving you flavor,
> So you can mix with spices and rice
> and be the lovely vitality of a human being.
> Remember when you drank rain in the garden.
> That was for this.

The chickpea ends up saying to the cook,

> You're my Cook, my Driver,
> My Way into Existence. I love your cooking.[47]

And as if that were not graphic enough, Rumi himself takes the place of the pea in another more uncompromising statement of what the soul undergoes in esoteric education: "I was raw; I was cooked; I was burnt."

167

By such routes we can enter into some appreciation of the nature of the alchemical work. The human being is the vessel, "learning to bear the beams of love," as Blake wrote. Love the agent, we the patients. Love the active, we the passive, until in turn we respond in activity to what was received in passivity. Love the necessary, we the contingent. But the inner meaning of infusion, just like the inner meanings of ecology and quantum physics and their different modes, is that these contraries do not exist as separations but as love-relationships, attractions, affinities. In the collapsed language or closed circle of sacred grammar this is even to be discovered:

> When the seeker has been found he looks through the eyes of his child and sees the secrets of his own heart.[48]

The parent does this, so does God, so does the lover. But as Coleridge knew, as well as the Tibetan masters, there is no way to come to love without being love itself. "From the soul itself," he said, the luminous cloud must come. As we have had reason to say elsewhere, a house cannot be explored from the outside only.

POETRY AND THE
SCIENCE OF WHOLENESS

THE DEEPEST INTERESTS of the Romantics converge, as we have seen, with the issues closest to present-day students of the spiritual traditions and holistic and ecological perspectives. But, with distinguished exceptions, little has been written to connect the world of the arts directly with the core teachings of the esoteric tradition. Throughout this book I have tried to show that the basic principles of esoteric work lie invisibly behind, and indeed generate and inform, some of the statements of Romantic poets whose writing is often thought to be beyond rational comprehension. These statements in poetry and prose have perplexed or been lost on a culture that has increasingly—until the advent of the new sciences and influx of teaching and teachers from other parts of the world—ignored the spiritual and esoteric dimension, tying itself to the social, historical, and material issues, from which point of view the Romantic poets indeed appear "not of this world." That is in a sense true: the esoteric tradition offers a facility to navigate the territory not covered by materialist and rationalist cartographers of myths and poems.

This territory, a region of creative action known by various names, is unmistakable as the world of Imagination in which spiritual facts formulate themselves intelligibly to the human predisposed, by creative activity or by meditation, to receive them. The region in which poetic metaphor functions has an intimate relation with the region "neither of heaven nor of earth" in which visionary experience occurs in spiritual practice. In this way, metaphor and esoteric work both stress the experiential mode essential to poetic imagination, whether this concerns the poet, reader, interpreter, teacher or seeker. Imagination can be known only by its like, participating in the matter, not only observing it.

All the foregoing essays in spiritual hermeneutics have been intended to take the principle of the imaginal realm, the *mundus imaginalis*, further into a modern context, and also to introduce it into a debate now emerging in literary studies as eco-criticism. The Romantics were the first substantial group of poets to imagine the relation of self to landscape and environment as a personal encounter, and the themes traced in the previous chapters concern the *plane* of this encounter, a plane determined not by optics but by soul. An urgent need to review the fundamentals of the relationship between human and environment is what raised "green issues" into consciousness in the first place. In this sense the Romantics were recalling a long-held secret of the esoteric "human sciences," not inventing a new one.

Ecology is the science of wholeness. Its detractors, stressing it is not the only perspective in science, give the ecological perspective "soft" status because it is not in their terms "objective"—any proof of the existence of an infinite web of interrelationships must of necessity include the dynamics of the proof and of its expounder. However, the environmental debate has tended to take the more pragmatic line of diagnosing the failure of ecosystems, and damage to the biosphere in general, as an effect of humans' ignoring the existence of such systems. The lesson of the rise of ecology could be summed up as the revelation of our capacity or incapacity to understand disaster resulting from ignorance. The arts have a similar revelation to make about an inner disaster which parallels the outer to an extraordinary degree. And this revelation of a negative implies a corresponding positive: a revolution of consciousness for which culture, not only science, economics, and politics, holds the potential.

Here the practical science of ecology touches the physical, philosophical, and metaphysical at once. Where traditional scientific perspective sees discrete units, bodies, and things, thereby corresponding with Cartesian notions of subject/object, self/other,[1] ecological perspective presents only a totality in which the "things" we are conditioned to see as autonomous entities are in fact interexistents.[2] Since humanity is now in charge of so much more of the natural environment that was the case even fifty years ago, the question of how we are educated to see our own identity and agency is more and more crucially invasive of the ground of our influence; for as a person thinks, so he or she will act. This is the argument for suggesting, as for example the Temenos Academy[3] has done, that the now evident enough damage to the biosphere is nothing other than a modality of an already long-standing damage to our idea of who we are and of what humanity is.

This already long-standing damage is done by what has been called the "Hypnosis of positivism,"[4] the conditioning power of the dominant edifice of Western philosophical tradition, which monopolizes subjectivity to the point where, at best by silent exclusion of other perspectives, at worst by out-and-out dismissal of them, only the post-Cartesian idea of self subsists in our culture.[5] It is well known that at this level the traditional scientific viewpoint has been one and the same as the empirical tradition in philosophy, so that when Richard Dawkins, for example, speaks of facts, he implies facts of science and facts of mind with the same term. It is only slowly becoming known that the ecological perspective, while accepting the veracity of visible results, also shares the channel of the esoteric tradition, a tradition which Toshihiko Isutzu has called a "metaphilosophy of oriental philosophies."[6]

———

171

Cartesian mindsets are profoundly unecological. The Cartesian irreducible is *I am here, the world is out there, and never the twain shall meet*, never, that is, other than in terms of incomprehension, hostility, manipulation, subjugation. Even Deism, a theological Cartesianism, a half-way house to Atheism[7] but unable to determine itself completely, placed God at a distance literally hopeless, spatially, and ontologically. This pessimistic slant makes it seem all but inevitable that the influence of the Cartesian world-picture should result in harmful physical effects in the environment. I think one can go further still and suggest that, for the Cartesian mind-set, the term "other" shades swiftly into the term "alien." For the unknowable other, studied so avidly by the existentialists, is alien in its unknowableness (like the seventeenth century Deity) and inspires not only perplexity but fear and disgust. The tunnel of alienation ends abruptly, soon enough, with the thought: What is unknowably alien might conceivably kill me. Therefore it is up to the subject and a community of subjects subscribing to enlightened self-interest to evolve means of self-protection, management of other, even deceit in order to preserve the identity shored up and bolstered as the Western Subject in its small glory. These means of protection are twin-armed in the normal description of subjectivity-in-society that we have inherited from the nineteenth and early twentieth century; one arm is technology, the other arm our definition of self, the humanist ego-identity. This situation is the inner disaster I referred to above. Where ecology has exposed the demonic character of technology,[8] so mysticism reveals that it is futile to rely on the salvific capacity of humanist ego-identity.[9]

Language, when used in metaphoric ways, in the usual preserve of poetry and poetic utterance, acts as an intersection of modes of consciousness that are far from Cartesian and very closely related to the ecological perspective. (It will be apparent of course that it is, strictly speaking, redundant for ecologists to argue that two things are related, for their axiom is that everything is already related to everything else and does not need an announcement to that effect. But not all discussion is carried out from ecological axioms for the reasons already given, and my intention has been to enable a dialogue to ensue between positions all too often thought to be mutually exclusive.) I hope this esoteric account of poetic language might also explain why, in all likelihood, the ubiquitous traditional divide between empirical consciousness and poetic consciousness has arisen. A holistic perspective, in the eyes of a dualist or Cartesian, is a direct threat to the autonomy of Cartesian identity, to its sense of isolation and containment, to its sense of uneasy détente, that between imprisonment in self on the one hand, and on the other, the safety of existing in a sealed container. For the dualist Western subject, poetic consciousness is therefore deeply attractive (for its promise of liberation from containment) and profoundly dangerous (because it collapses the protective walls of the self-container). It is no coincidence that the characteristics of the dualist Western subject are so close to the features of paranoid consciousness, which seeks to contain and control the forces which it finds most alluring.

The ecological perspective, the poetic perspective, and mysticism share an identical principle: the absolute unity of existence.[10] The western mind has had great trouble seeing its way to this fundamental correspondence, and my particular suggestion here is that it is perhaps only poetry—or the operations of consciousness that correspond to poetry's action— that can help to mediate the gulf that has eventuated between mysticism and the Western humanist mind-set. Domiciliaries of Western consciousness have argued that to accept the absolute unity of existence is to sacrifice the diverse realities of the world, inner and outer, subsuming them all into a kind of mush. This judgement is usually implicit in the attribution of pantheism. Moral reverberations begin to surface too, such that the Oneness of existence is generally seen to be the preserve of new agers, cloudy mystics, Platonists, lazy thinkers, or, at this judgement's utmost of generosity, as the origin of a technique by which relaxation therapists delude their clients into calming down. In these views, we can feel, as it were tamed for the humanist audience, all the remonstrations rooted in ideas of hard versus soft science, and there, for many people and many intellectual communities, discussion of mysticism or metaphysics ends. For a Cartesian viewpoint, in order that justice be done to the diversity of experience and things, each "thing" must be declared self-subsistent, a substantive (as nouns used to be called). By corollary each human self is deemed similar to a substantive—independent, self-subsistent, autonomous. And again here the moral overtones accumulate, only this time positively. Independence, self-subsistence, autonomy are cast not only as humanist virtues, but virtually as human rights. If you like, *thing* and *self* enjoy a holy pact for the duration of the Western humanist age, and mutually support each other in its discourses.

But the advent of ecology, plus the increasing tide of interest in Buddhist, Hindu, and Islamic metaphysics through more and better translations, is making it clear that a true experience of wholeness, of the unity of existence, doesn't in the slightest diminish our capacity to appreciate the variety and diversity of the world. Far from acting the deliquescent and reducing diversity into an ill-conceived "blur" of oneness, it creates a state of awareness in which all the things of the world and the multiplicity of human response to those things are seen to be inter-related, not as existing in precarious and proud isolation, not, if you like, in the hubris of thingness. Ecology has done much to make graphic evidence available. Sustained observations of ecosystems actually bring us into closer specific relationship with individual animal and plant species, and mineral, chemical, and organic processes, such that their specific character is highlighted, at the same time as being acknowledged to be essentially interexistent, the factorial aspect of a living system, an aspect limited in manifestation to its own dimension, but not limited by its own dimension.

The theory of holarchy and the holon put forward by Koestler and others[11] is the "seeding" argument here in this transition of world-picture from Cartesian to Ecological. No thing is correctly regarded if it's regarded as a free-standing thing. In one important sense there is nothing that can correctly be regarded as a thing at all.

This is precisely where poetry enters the picture again. The metaphorical mode natural and typical in poetic language proposes, as a fact of nature and a fact of mind, that we can speak of one thing in terms of another, and not do violence to either. Indeed what ecology and mysticism indicate along with poetry is that the poetic mode of speaking of one thing in terms of another is actually physically and metaphysically more accurate than the old Aristotelian saying of logic, to the effect that a thing cannot be both itself and not itself at the same time. However, the proposition of poetic language and of mysticism, that a thing not only can be both itself and not itself but is so in the nature of things (more nearly, in the nature of nature), is so unfamiliar to a post-Empiricist mind-set that it is seen as virtual nonsense, if it is considered at all. The concept of the holon instead of the thing lets us see this. It intimates to us the symbolic character of all perception, a fact recorded by Coleridge in great detail and with apparent prescience of the ecological world-view.[12] It also gives another instance of Wittgenstein's paradoxical saying that all descriptions are misdescriptions (if they purport to one referent object only) and that the only valid seeing is "seeing as."[13]

The intersection between mysticism, ecological perspective, and poetic metaphor, and the usefulness of noticing that

intersection, is caught *in vivo* by studying the different implications of the two statements

  i) The flower of the plant species *rosa canina* exists
  [is existing, is existent]
                            and
  ii) Existence flowers as the species *rosa canina.*

According to ecology and esoteric tradition, only the second
of these two statements, *Existence flowers as* rosa canina, offers a
metaphysically accurate grammar, where, existence being one
and a unity, it must of necessity be the subject, not the predicate. Now to say this is not immediately to import the Judaeo-
Christian transcendental signifier, as many feminists and post-
structuralists have assumed. It does not imply that the existence that is one and unique is male, or a father, or an angry
father in the sky; what it does imply is that it is one and a
whole, not one and another. Since it cannot be another, then
what it might appear from an outward view to be—i.e.,
another, a free-standing thing, in this case the dog-rose—may
not stand in the position of the one and only existence, which
ought to be the subject, if grammar is to conform to ontology.
This, as we saw in chapter 2, is the metaphysical meaning of
the *shahadah* or confession of Islam, *la illaha ill'allah* [There is
no reality but the one reality[14]], discussed in Islamic countries
amongst mystics of the school of *wahdat al wujud.*[15]
  What poetry, more nearly poetic metaphor, does, without
depending on theological or logical arguments and discourses,
is to live or breathe the air of this one unique existent, without
naming itself as that, but rather able to intimate to the perceiv-
ing reader or hearer the basic relatedness (as related to itself)
of all the different things of which it speaks, and of all others
besides. This is the special power of metaphor. Islamic metaphysics calls it the breath of existentiation (*nafas ar rahman*). It

is essential that this metaphysical ground-consciousness is not named for the reader of the poem. Like breathed air, it is essentially invisible and equally essentially vivifying. If it named itself as the one existent it would already have sacrificed its function of a consciousness that is sheer or pure to the extent that it is unnamed and unnamable but grants the possibility of existentiation to all that is named, descended, effused, declined—we can speak here equally of parts of speech, living beings, souls.

The significant fact about the existence of this ground-consciousness in metaphor is that, in its hiddenness, its power to enlarge our perspective beyond "thingness" is wholly non-sectarian. This power is of course described in the metaphysics of all world religions, and in such guises it is simply declining into a name, another locality, another metaphor. But in its real state it is invisible. As Shelley so effortlessly stated, "the deep truth is imageless."[16] And as we saw in chapter 5, Shelley's ode "To a Skylark" is more truly a metaphysical poem than any written by the seventeenth century English poets because it speaks this pure light, and of its "lamps" and "reflectors" in all the four worlds, down to the image of a bird in the here and now. But the metaphysics of imagination allow it to be certain that at the same time, "bird thou never wert."

When we read a poem like Shelley's ode, we find the holistic and mystical principle perfectly enacted, enacted perfectly to evade the Cartesian mind-set, avoiding as well the imprecision of reference with which mysticism is traditionally reproached by many academics. Any possibility of attributing the speaker or the protagonist is ruled out. But the actual proponent is the one unique existent that grounds all appearances and gives them reality beyond their incident forms, forms which if regarded alone without the breath of existentiation, would be, as the Buddhists say, wholly void and without reality.

Alchemy is another example of poetic / holistic / ecological consciousness that carried the non-Cartesian stream in Europe long before Eastern mysticism became remotely fashionable in the West (or again unfashionable, depending on the community whose opinions prevail). In the symbolic imagery of alchemy[17] we find that the ruling principle of a semantic ecosystem is interrelation of factors not mutually exclusive but englobed in one another. Gold functions in alchemical discourse equally as

> {the most precious and indestructible metal}
> {solidified sunlight}
> {the perfection of life}
> {the divine humanity}

Alchemy, like poetic language, is a symbolic language. All the processes it describes as happening in the alchemist's retort—combustion, convection, condensation, precipitation, the fixing of compounds, the processes of solution and coagulation—can be witnessed in the natural environment, and simultaneously they describe what is undergone by the human soul. Since alchemy was based in a holarchic picture of existence, it embodies (like homeopathy and herbal medicine) the law of similars. What occurs at one level (the form and ritual of the alchemical work—the oven, crucible, and retort) is hologrammed at the levels above (psyche, soul, spirit) and below (the natural environment). Alchemical thought brings us closer to the possibility of cosmos as metaphor, a view taken as axiomatic by eco-consciousness and mysticism. Each level simultaneously resounds with the event of transformation; with what the sinologist Hellmut Wilhelm translates as the concept of "change."[18]

From investigating poetic language from the point of view of ecology and mystical grammar, we may conclude that metaphor is a principled equivalence of signification, such that anyone using metaphor is involved at every stage in the proposition of one thing in terms of another, or of that other in terms of the one, or, more often than not, of the intersection without obvious priority of the two. In this sense metaphor is an effective refusal of the Aristotelian logic which denies that a thing can be both itself and not itself at the same time—on the contrary, metaphor affirms precisely that, in the simplest of terms, and enacts it whenever its use is so deliberate as not to invite its status to be designated "merely metaphorical." In many forms of poetry this principle can be witnessed in operation, when the ornamental function of metaphor gives way to the cognitive.[19] A prime example of the cognitive taking the place of ornamental is Plato's use of the extended metaphor of the winged soul in *Phaedrus.*

So poetic language is not merely a tactical means of representation implicating witness, witnessed, and audience, but an instancing of the fundamental principle of ecology, the interexistence as a whole of what appear to be separate beings to the unregenerated eye (the Cartesian eye whose errant brain the discipline of ecology evolved to educate). Language and world interexist at this pitch of description, in a manner I suggest is not widely apparent to contemporary thought, which normally insists the contrary. This is why the principle of "sacred grammar" known to metaphysics as the hypostatic declaration of unity, and to ecology as holarchic system, becomes relevant, and reverses the order of parts of speech such that existence is the substance, not the accident as it appears when falsely cast as a predicate. The examples of Shelley's "To a Skylark" (see chapter 5) and the equally miraculous "Ode to the West Wind" show that metaphor used in a certain way demonstrates that a thing can both be and not be at the same time, in the way demonstrated by ecology, and that its so being and not being does not deny its individuated existence but amplifies and validates it to a degree which makes obsolete the fearful marginalising of the Other, an exclusion that is the sole and unfortunate recourse of the Cartesian gifted (or plagued, as it might initially be put) with imagination; a recourse which he or she is forced to take until such time as the Cartesian mind-set is dissolved in favour of a holistic one.

Poetry, like alchemy, is a deed of imagination, and it is by direct use of this faculty of imagination that the ecological perspective sees beyond "things" to the holon, to the instancing of multiple related levels of cosmos in one particular aspect. Like mysticism, ecology and poetry are imaginative acts whose value is that they are the imaginal aspect of Being, not the imaginary invention of a deluded artist.

NOTES

INTRODUCTION

1. Shelley, *A Defence of Poetry*, ed. H. A. Needham, pp. 100, 101, 102.

2. Ibid., p. 109.

3. Matchett, *Journeys of Nothing in the Land of Everything*, p. 7.

4. Shelley, *Defence*, p. 109.

5. See David Bohm, *Unfolding Meaning*, chapters 1 and 2; also *Wholeness and the Implicate Order.*

6. A. Blake, *A Seminar on Time*, p. 123.

7. See Huston Smith, "Two Traditions–and Philosophy" in *Religion of the Heart*, eds. Nasr and Stoddart, pp. 278-96.

8. Idries Shah, *The Sufis*, p. 161.

9. William Blake, *The Last Judgement*, §1.

10. Peter Young, "The New," *Beshara* 6 (1988), p. 13.

11. Huston Smith, "Two Traditions–and Philosophy," op. cit., p. 283.

12. Ibid., p. 279.

13. Ibid.

14. Bohm, *Unfolding Meaning*, p. 8.

15. Idries Shah, *The Sufis*, p. 392.

CHAPTER 1

1. Wordsworth, "Ode: Intimations of Immortality," lines 56-7.

2. Coleridge, *Anima Poetae, Poems and Prose*, p. 139.

3. Gaston Bachelard, *The Poetics of Reverie*, p. 161; Ramana Maharshi, *Forty Verses on Reality*, invocation; Elémire Zolla, *Archetypes*, p. 75.

4. Dom Sylvester Houédard, "The Question about questions," *Beshara News Bulletin*, November 1986.

5. Kathleen Raine, *India Seen Afar*, p. 285.

6. Cf. Kathleen Raine, introduction to *Poet to Poet: Shelley*, p. 12.

7. See J. G. Bennett, *Needs of a New Age Community*, pp. 27-45, 67-73, 97-99.

8. See, for example, Do Ring, *The Urga Manuscript*, p. 7; Sri Krishna Menon, *Atma Darshan*, chapters 7, 11, 16, 17.

9. See Ibn 'Arabi, tr. T.H. Weir, *Whoso Knoweth Himself [Treatise on Unity]*, pp. 20-24; Henry Corbin, *Spiritual Body and Celestial Earth*, p. 61.

10. Elémire Zolla, *Archetypes*, p. 75.

11. Coleridge, "Dejection: an Ode"; Wordsworth, "Ode: Intimations of Immortality." Cf. Tennyson's poems "Tears, Idle Tears" and "Break, break, break," also Christopher Ricks, *Tennyson: A Biography*, p. 14.

12. Dom Sylvester Houédard, "The Question about Questions," part 2, *Beshara* I, p.7.

13. Anthony Blake, *A Seminar on Time*, pp. 171-3.

14. Idries Shah, *The Sufis*, p. 392.

15. Zolla, *Archetypes*, p. 34.

16. In conversation with the author at Chisholme House, 1992.

17. Henry Corbin, *Spiritual Body and Celestial Earth*, p. 226.

18. See Zolla, *Archetypes*, p. 33; Do Ring, *The Urga Manuscript*, p. 9.

19. See Richard Holmes, *Shelley: The Pursuit*, pp. 17, 24-5, 44-5, 65-6.

20. Coleridge, *Biographia Literaria*, Chapter 13, *Poems and Prose*, p. 191.

21. Arthur Koestler, *The Roots of Coincidence*, p. 100.

22. Alan Watts, *The Two Hands of God*, pp. 11-12.

23. Owen Barfield, *Poetic Diction*, p. 20.

24. A.E.I. Falconar, *Sufi Literature and the Journey to Immortality*, p. 167.

25. Shelley, Fragments connected with "Epipsychidion," II.141-5, *Poetical Works*, ed. Hutchinson, p. 423.

26. Dom Sylvester Houédard, op. cit. p. 7.

27. Coleridge, *Anima Poetae, Poems and Prose*, p. 141. See also Ibn 'Arabi, *Fusus al Hikam*, tr. Ralph Austin, pp. 145-54, 188, 192-3, 257; Fakhruddin Iraqi, tr. P. Lamborn Wilson, *Divine Flashes*, p. 65 n.2; Zolla, *Archetypes*, pp. 18-19.

28. See Anthony Blake, *A Seminar on Time*, pp. 108-9.

29. Dom Sylvester Houédard, "The Question about Questions," op. cit. p. 7 (my italics).

30. Ibid.

31. Quoted by Corbin, *Creative Imagination in the Sufism of Ibn 'Arabi)*, p. 382.

CHAPTER 2

1. Benz, *Mystical Sources of German Romantic Philosophy*, p. 21.

2. Shelley, "On Life," *Essays & Letters*, p. 72.

3. Coleridge, *The Friend; Poetry and Prose*, p. 157.

4. Ibid., p. 158.

5. Ibid.

6. W.B. Yeats, "The Autumn of the Body," *Selected Criticism*, p. 41.

7. Thomas Merton, *Zen and the Birds of Appetite*, p. 163.

8. See Anthony Blake, *A Seminar on Time*, pp. 111-18, 136-7, 161-2.

9. William Blake, *The Last Judgement*, § 1 and 2.

10. See J.G. Bennett, *Deeper Man*, chapter 10.

11. Coleridge, op. cit. p. 157.

12. See E.G. Howe, *The Mind of the Druid*, p. 135; Schlemmer and Jenkins (eds), *The Only Planet of Choice*, p. 75.

13. Howe, op. cit., p. 135.

14. *Kathopanishad*, tr. J. Mascaro, *The Upanishads*, p. 64; see also Claude Bragdon, *The Eternal Poles*, chapter 6.

15. Howe, op. cit., pp. 132-3. See also Frithjof Schuon, *Sufism: Veil and Quintessence*, chapter 7. See also David Bohm, *Unfolding Meaning*, p. 155, and Schlemmer and Jenkins (eds.), *The Only Planet of Choice*, p. 81; and Sri Atmananda, *Atma Darshan*, p. 1.

16. Elémire Zolla, *Archetypes*, p. 33.

17. Coleridge, *Anima Poetae, Poems and Prose*, p.143; *Biographia Literaria*, Chapter XIII.

18. William Blake, *Poems*, p. 362.

19. Henry Corbin, *Avicenna and the Visionary Recital*, p. 20.

20. Ibn 'Arabi), *Futuhat al Makkiyah*; Nasr and Stoddart (eds.), *Religion of the Heart*, p. 69.

21. See Ernest Benz, *Mystical Sources of German Romantic Philosophy*, pp. 74-5, 94, 99.

22. David Bohm, *Unfolding Meaning*, p. 155, offers illuminating further comment.

23. See A. Affifi, commentary to Ibn 'Arabi), *Fusus al Hikam*, p. 105.

24. Shelley, *Prometheus Unbound*, III. 4. line 204.

25. Coleridge, *Table Talk*, June 23 1834, p. 265.

26. See Ernest Benz, op. cit., p. 23.

27. Elémire Zolla, op. cit., p. 33.

28. Ibid.

29. See Schuon, *Sufism: Veil and Quintessence*, chapter 7.

30. Corbin, *The Man of Light in Iranian Sufism*, pp 106, 118.

31. Zolla, op. cit., p. 34.

32. Ibid., p. 35. See also Donald Lopez, *The Heart Sutra Explained: Indian and Tibetan Commentaries*, p. 55, and Ramana Maharshi, *The Spiritual Teaching of Ramana Maharshi*, pp. 4, 87.

33. Quoted in *Temenos* 9 (1988), p. 53.

34. Shakespeare, *Richard II*, V. v.

35. Coleridge, *Table Talk*, Nov 3 1833, p. 244.

36. See J. G. Bennett, *Deeper Man*, pp. 164-5; 212-33.

37. Elémire Zolla, op. cit., p. 4.

38. Hermann Raschke, *Der Innere Logos im Antiken und Deutschen Idealismus*, p. 76. (my translation).

39. See O. M. Aivanhov, *Aquarius*, pp. 230-237.

40. See Jonathan Cott, *Stockhausen: Conversations with the Composer*, p. 149.

41. Rumi, tr. Coleman Barks, *Delicious Laughter*, pp. 64-5

42. Henry Corbin, *Spiritual Body and Celestial Earth*, pp. 54, 57.

43. Jakob Böhme, ed. R. Waterfield, *Selected Writings*, p. 224.

44. D. L. Snellgrove (ed.), *The Nine Ways of Bon*, p. 243.

CHAPTER 3

1. Coleridge, *Poems and Prose*, p. 126.

2. Ajahn Sumedho, *Mind and the Way*, p. 212.

3. Gaston Bachelard, *The Poetics of Reverie*, p. 162.

4. Hermann Raschke, *Der Innere Logos im Antiken und Deutschen Idealismus*, pp. 54, 60.

5. See Ernest Benz, *The Mystical Sources of German Romantic Philosophy*, chapters 3 and 5.

6. Arthur Koestler, *The Roots of Coincidence*, p. 128.

7. Rudolf Steiner, *Secrets of the Threshold*, Lecture V. See also "Lectures to the Arbeitsgemeinschaft, 1921."

8. See Koestler, op. cit., p. 100.

9. Elémire Zolla, *Archetypes*, p. 66.

10. William Wordsworth, Preface to the *Lyrical Ballads*.

11. Samuel Beckett, *How It Is*, p. 104.

———

12. Zolla, op. cit., p. 1.

13. "A Speculation about Landscape," *Cambridge Quarterly*, vol. 6, No. 4 (1975), p. 65.

14. Huxley, *Island*, pp. 212-215, 301.

15. Coleridge, *Poems and Prose*, p. 141.

16. Quoted in Henry Corbin, *Spiritual Body and Celestial Earth*, p. 27.

17. Ibid., p. 86.

18. Ibid., p. 30.

19. Ibid., p. 82.

20. Namkhai Norbu Rinpoche, ed. J. Shane, *Dzogchen*, p. 53.

21. Koestler, op. cit., pp. 108, 149.

22. Huston Smith, "Two Traditions–and Philosophy," in Nasr and Stoddart (eds), *Religion of the Heart*, pp. 279-83.

23. See Corbin, op. cit., p. 213.

24. See Corbin, "The Stranger and the Guide," in *Avicenna and the Visionary Recital*, p. 16.

25. See Corbin, *Spiritual Body and Celestial Earth*, p. 66; *Creative Imagination in the Sufism of Ibn 'Arabi.* chapter 3, parts 1 and 2; Arthur Versluis, "The True Postmodernism," *Temenos* 13 (1992), pp. 216-31; David Mitchell, "Nature as Theophany," *Temenos* 7 (1986), pp. 84-114; Kathleen Raine, "Nature, House of the Soul," *Temenos* 9 (1988), pp. 251-68.

26. Corbin, *Spiritual Body and Celestial Earth*, p. 83.

27. G. Bachelard, *The Poetics of Reverie*, p. 161.

28. Coleridge, "The Aeolian Harp," *Poems and Prose*, p. 30.

29. Ibid., 11.39-42.

30. Coleridge, "This Lime-Tree Bower My Prison," *Poetry and Prose*, p. 34.

31. Coleridge, op. cit. p. 34.

32. Bachelard, *The Poetics of Reverie*, p. 200.

33. Coleridge, *Poetry and Prose*, pp. 94-98.

34. Coleridge, "Frost At Midnight," *Poetry and Prose*, pp. 74-75 (my italics).

35. Bachelard, *The Poetics of Reverie*, p. 200.

36. Corbin, *Spiritual Body and Celestial Earth*, p. 29. See also p 104.

37. Ibn 'Arabi, *Futuhat al Makkiyah*, quoted in Corbin, *Spiritual Body and Celestial Earth*, p. 137.

38. Coleridge, "This Lime-Tree Bower My Prison," 11.39-41, *Poetry and Prose*, pp. 34-6.

39. See Do Ring, ed. George Hall, *The Urga Manuscript*, and Corbin, "Harmonic Perception," *Spiritual Body, Celestial Earth*, p. 51.
40. Coleridge, "On Having left a Place of Retirement," 11.63-4.
41. See H. Corbin, *Avicenna and the Visionary Recital*, pp. 28-35.
42. K. Okakura, *The Book of Tea*, p. 87.
43. See Richard MacEwan, "The Ecological Theatre and the Evolutionary Play," *Beshara News Bulletin*, November 1986, pp. 3-6.
44. Anthony Blake, *A Seminar on Time*, p. 69.

CHAPTER 4

1. Coleridge, "Anima Poetae," *Poetry and Prose*, p. 141.
2. Harold Bloom, *The Anxiety of Influence*.
3. Ibn 'Arabi, *Futuhat al Makkiyah* IV, 279.7, quoted in Nasr and Stoddart (eds.), *Religion of the Heart*, p. 80.
4. See Ernest Benz, *The Mystical Sources of German Romantic Philosophy*, chapters 2, 4, and 5; James Webb, *The Harmonious Circle*, Part 3, Chapter 1.
5. Idries Shah, *The Sufis*, p. 161.
6. See Kathleen Raine, *Coleridge*, p. 30; Abd al Karim al Jili, tr. T. Burckhardt, *Universal Man*, introduction; Abraham Abadi, "A Consideration of Anthropocentrism," *Beshara* 2 (Summer 1987), pp. 8-10.
7. Kathleen Raine, *Coleridge*, p. 29.
8. See H. Raschke, *Der Innere Logos im Antiken und Deutschen Idealismus*, pp. 60, 76; Jili, *Universal Man*, Chapter 1.
9. See Burckhardt, *Universal Man*, p. 5; Paul J. Lin, (tr. and ed.), *Tao Te Ching*, I.
10. T. L. Rampa, *You Forever*, p. 140.
11. K. Raine, *Coleridge*, p. 31.
12. G. M. Hopkins, *Poems and Prose*, letter no. II, p. 153.
13. See Owen Barfield, *Poetic Diction*, chapters 1, 2, 12; Appendix IV.
14. Keats, "Ode To a Nightingale," *Poems*, pp. 346-348.
15. Anthony Blake, *A Seminar On Time*, p. 137; J. G. Bennett, *Deeper Man*, pp. 121-123.
16. See the "Verticalist Manifesto" in D. McMillan, *Transition 1927-38*, p. 66; Kathleen Raine, "The Vertical," *Temenos* 13 (1992), pp. 195-212.
17. See P. D. Ouspensky, *The Psychology of Man's Possible Evolution*, pp. 57-60.

18. H. Corbin, *Spiritual Body and Celestial Earth*, p. 3.

19. Corbin, *Creative Imagination in the Sufism of Ibn 'Arabi; Cyclical Time and Ismaili Gnosis; Spiritual Body and Celestial Earth: Mazdean Iran to Shiite Iran; Avicenna and the Visionary Recital; The Man of Light in Iranian Sufism.*

20. Corbin, *Spiritual Body and Celestial Earth*, pp. 10-11.

21. Ibid., pp. 11-12.

22. Coleridge, Letter to John Thelwall, *Poetry and Prose*, p. 132.

23. Coleridge, "Appendix, Lay Sermon" in *The Stateman's Manual*, (*Biographia Literaria* and *Lay Sermons*).

24. Coleridge, *Biographia Literaria.*

25. Ibid., ch. IV.

26. Ibid.

27. Ibid., ch. X.

28. Ibid., ch. XIII.

29. See Aldous Huxley, *The Doors of Perception*, pp. 24-33, 38-40, 73-86.

30. Coleridge, *Table Talk*, Aug. 20 1833.

31. Coleridge, "Appendix, Lay Sermon" in *The Stateman's Manual*. (*Biographia Literaria* and *Lay Sermons*).

32. See Henry Corbin, "The Jasmine of the Fedeli d'Amore," *Sphinx* 3, (1990), pp. 189-223; *Creative Imagination in the Sufism of Ibn 'Arabi*, pp. 136-144.

33. Corbin, *Creative Imagination*, p. 163.

34. Corbin, *Avicenna and the Visionary Recital*, p. 196.

35. Coleridge, "Anima Poetae," *Poetry and Prose*, p. 139.

CHAPTER 5

1. Henry Corbin, *Creative Imagination in the Sufism of Ibn 'Arabi*, p. 180.

2. Anthony Blake, *A Seminar on Time*, p. 79.

3. David Bohm, *Wholeness and the Implicate Order; Unfolding Meaning: A Dialogue with David Bohm*. See also J. G. Bennett, *Existence (Dramatic Universe Series No. 2)*, pp. 43ff.

4. Bennett, *Deeper Man*, p. 233.

5. Shelley, *A Defence of Poetry. Essays and Letters*, p. 33.

6. Blake, *The Marriage of Heaven and Hell. Poems*, p. 132.

7. E. G. Howe, *The Mind of the Druid*, p. 12.

8. Coleridge, "Psyche," *Poetry and Prose*, p. 105.

9. See Kathleen Raine, *Blake and Antiquity,* plate 25.

10. Cf. Llewellyn Vaughan-Lee, *The Call and the Echo,* p. 33.

11. Cf. Chögyam Trungpa, *Meditation in Action,* pp. 32, 89-90, 111.

12. J. G. Bennett, *Deeper Man,* p. 232. See also Ibn 'Arabi, *The Kernel of the Kernel,* pp. 23-24.

13. J. G. Bennett, *Deeper Man,* p. 232.

14. Shelley, *A Defence of Poetry. Essays and Letters,* p. 33.

15. See Ibn 'Arabi, tr. and ed. R. Austin, *Fusus al Hikam,* chapters 2, 12, 15, 16, l9, 24, 25, 27.

16. J. G. Bennett, *Deeper Man,* pp. l27-8.

17. William Blake, "There Is No Natural Religion." *Poems,* p. l5.

18. See: J. G. Bennett, *The Dramatic Universe Series,* vol. 3, chapters 1 and 4; *The Tibetan Book of the Dead,* ed. and tr. Fremantle and Trungpa; Henry Corbin, *Spiritual Body and Celestial Earth,* pp. 53-60, 129.

19. Anthony Blake, *A Seminar on Time,* p. l09.

20. Ibid., p. 112.

21. J. G. Bennett, *Deeper Man,* pp. l21-3.

22. See C.G. Jung, *Synchronicity,* pp. 7-10.

23. Anthony Blake, op. cit., p. 151.

24. Arthur Koestler, *The Roots of Coincidence,* p. 122.

25. See, for other examples: Owen Barfield, *Romanticism Comes of Age,* p. 67; Kathleen Raine, *Golgonooza, City of Imagination,* pp. 57-8, 76; Sogyal Rinpoche, *The Tibetan Book of Living and Dying,* pp. 11-12, 102, 103-4, 107-8, 274-75; D.L. Snellgrove, *The Nine Ways of Bon,* p. 11; Henry Corbin, *Spiritual Body, Celestial Earth,* p. 11, 176; Paracelsus, ed. N. Goodrick-Clarke, *Essential Readings,* pp. 45, 47-49, 112, 113, 117.

26. See Sogyal Rinpoche, op. cit., pp. 343-349, 352; Robert M. Pirsig, *Lila: An Enquiry into Morals,* pp. 393-97.

27. See, for example: Gershom Scholem, *Zohar,* p. 29; *Ismail Hakki Bursevi's translation of and commentary on Ibn 'Arabi, Fusus al Hikam,* tr. Bulent Rauf, vol. 1, pp. 24-26, 92, 153, 253; Kathleen Raine, *Golgonooza, City of Imagination,* pp. 36, 39; Henry Corbin, *Spiritual Body and Celestial Earth,* pp. 55-60; 130, 208, 244.

28. Anthony Blake, op. cit., p. 156. See also Rudolf Steiner, *Illness and Death, The Origins of Evil, and The Origin of Suffering,* pp. 10-13.

29. Goethe, *Farbenlehre,* introduction.

30. Gershom Scholem, *Zohar,* p. 29.

31. Anthony Blake, op. cit., p. 118.

32. J.G. Bennett, *Deeper Man*, p. 237.

33. See Coleridge, *Biographia Literaria*, chapter VIII; E.G. Howe, *The Mind of the Druid*, pp. 124-5.

34. See Sri Atmananda, *Atma Darshan*, chapters 7, 16, 17, 20.

35. Wittgenstein, *Tractatus Logico-Philosophicus*, final proposition.

36. See David Bohm, *Unfolding Meaning*, p. 165.

37. Peter Lamborn Wilson, introduction to Fakhruddin Iraqi, *Divine Flashes*, p. 8.

38. Peter Lamborn Wilson, op. cit., introduction, p. 7.

39. On *Dharmakaya* see Herbert Guenther, *Meditation Differently*, pp. 9, 23 n. 8, 38.

40. See A. Affifi, commentary on *Fusus al Hikam*, p. 105.

41. M. Spiegelman (ed.), *Sufism, Islam and Jungian Psychology*, p. 113.

42. Henry Corbin, *Creative Imagination*, p. 192.

43. Ibid., pp. 270-271.

44. M. Spiegelman, op. cit., p. 111.

45. J.G. Bennett, *Deeper Man*, p. 128.

46. J. Nurbakhsh, *Traditions of the Prophet*, p. 57; Ibn 'Arabi, *Kernel of the Kernel*, p. 10.

47. See Nasr and Stoddart (eds.), *Religion of the Heart*, pp. 60, 77; Peter Lamborn Wilson and William Chittick (eds), *Divine Flashes*, pp. 22, 65n; Sogyal Rinpoche, op. cit., p. 26; Ibn 'Arabi, tr. R. Austin, *Bezels of Wisdom*, chapters 12, 16, 25.

48. See Fritjof Capra, *The Tao of Physics*, chapters 12 and 13.

49. Ibn 'Arabi, *Kernel of the Kernel*, p. 12

50. William Blake, *The Marriage of Heaven and Hell; The Last Judgement*.

51. Al-Ghazzali, ed. and tr. M. Hazarvi, *Mysteries of the Human Soul*, p. 46.

52. William Blake, *The Last Judgement; Milton*, Book I.

CHAPTER 6

1. Plato, *Republic*, tr Rieu, part 11; Edouard Schuré, *The Great Initiates*, chapters 16-18, 36, 37.

2. Alvin Moore, "Insouciant Birds" in *Religion of the Heart: a Festschrift for Frithjof Schuon*, eds. Nasr and Stoddart, p. 232.

3. See Ibn 'Arabi, tr. Bulent Rauf, *Kernel of the Kernel*, pp. 20-21.

4. See A.E.I. Falconar, *Sufi Literature and the Journey to Immortality*, p. 6.

5. See Christopher Ricks, *Tennyson,* pp. 12-15, 61-62, 189-191.

6. Keats, *Letters,* ed. H. E. Rollins, vol. 1, pp. 102-103.

7. Coleridge, "Dejection: an Ode," lines 54-55.

8. See Richard Holmes, *Shelley: The Pursuit,* pp. 24, 37, 41, 44-46, 149-150, 506-507, 604.

9. Samuel Beckett, *Proust and Three Dialogues,* pp. 18-29, 42-3, 63.

10. Shelley, *A Defence of Poetry. Essays and Letters,* pp. 11, 32.

11. Jampa Thaye [David Stott], *A Circle of Protection for the Unborn,* p. 11.

12. Llewellyn Vaughan-Lee, *The Call and the Echo,* p. 157.

13. Henry Corbin, *Avicenna and the Visionary Recital,* p. 19.

14. Wordsworth, "Ode: Intimations of Immortality," lines 163-168.

15. Wordsworth, "Ode: Intimations of Immortality," Stanza VI.

16. See: P. D. Ouspensky, *In Search of the Miraculous,* pp. 143-5, 217-20; Jean Vaysse, *Toward Awakening,* pp. 131-156; G. I. Gurdjieff, *Life is real only then, when "I am"* (Third Series), pp. 19-25, 131-139, 143-147.

17. Corbin, *Avicenna,* p. 20.

18. Coleridge, *Poems and Prose,* pp. 139-141.

19. Corbin, *Avicenna,* p. 20.

20. Ernest Benz, *The Mystical Sources of German Romantic Philosophy,* chapters 1, 4, and 5.

21. Corbin, *Avicenna,* p. 20.

22. Ibid., p. 21.

23. See Corbin, *Spiritual Body and Celestial Earth,* pp. 13ff, 24-30, 45ff; *Avicenna,* pp. 5, 15, 35-50.

24. Wordsworth, "Ode: Intimations of Immortality," lines 164, 167-8.

25. See Ibn 'Arabi, *Fusus al Hikam,* tr. Ralph Austin, pp. 111-118, 163-171, 198-205, 249-266.

26. Ibn 'Arabi, *Futuhat al Makkiyah* II 160-161, quoted in *Religion of the Heart,* eds. Nasr and Stoddart, p. 59.

27. Ibn 'Arabi, *Futuhat* I.287.19, quoted in Nasr and Stoddart, op. cit., p. 59.

28. See Akhtar Qamber, "The Mirror Symbol in the Teachings and Writings of Some Sufi Masters," *Temenos* 11, pp. 63-80.

29 Corbin, *Avicenna* p. 20.

30. Zolla, *Archetypes,* p. 11.

31. Corbin, *Avicenna,* p. 20.

32. Zolla, *Archetypes,* p. 4.

33. Ibid., p. 4. (my italics).

CHAPTER 7

1. See Huston Smith, "Two Traditions–and Philosophy," in Nasr and Stoddart (eds.), *Religion of the Heart*, pp. 278-296.

2. Gaston Bachelard, *The Poetics of Reverie*, chapter 5.

3. Quoted by J. P. Russo, "Dialogues with Deities," *Times Literary Supplement*, May 2nd, 1975.

4. Coleridge, "On Method," *The Friend*, vol. 1 Essay XI, (My italics).

5. Quoted in Richard Holmes, *Shelley: The Pursuit*, p. 295.

6. Lawrence Blair, *Rhythms of Vision*, p. 184.

7. See Ibn 'Arabi, tr. T. H. Weir, "*Whoso Knoweth Himself...*," pp. 4-5, 7, 16-17, 26.

8. See Samuel Beckett, *Proust and Three Dialogues*, p. 123; see also *The Twenty-Nine Pages*, pp. 4-18.

9. For example, Kakuzo Okakura, *The Book of Tea*, pp. 27-28, 35-37, 43-45.

10. Rudolf Steiner, *Knowledge of Higher Worlds*, pp. 45-55, 104-116; *Occult Science: an Outline*, pp. 228-233.

11. D. H. Lawrence, *Psychoanalysis and the Unconscious*, chapters 2, 3, 5, and 6.

12. See, for example, Titus Burckhardt, *Alchemy*; Corbin, *Spiritual Body and Celestial Earth*, pp. 97-101; *Avicenna and the Visionary Recital*, pp. 208-221.

13. William Blake, *Jerusalem*, chapter 4.

14. Corbin, *Avicenna and the Visionary Recital*, p. 30.

15 Corbin, *Spiritual Body and Celestial Earth*, p. 213.

16. Coleridge, *The Statesman's Manual* quoted in Owen Barfield, *What Coleridge Thought*, p. 195.

17. A. E. I. Falconar, *Sufi Literature and the Journey to Immortality*, p. 6.

18. J. W. von Goethe, *Maximen und Reflexionen*, no. 488.

19. Corbin, *Avicenna*, p. 85.

20. Goethe, *Faust* II, lines 12104-8.

21. David Bohm, *Unfolding Meaning*, p. 152.

22. A. E. I. Falconar, op. cit., p. 6.

23. Corbin, *Creative Imagination in the Sufism of Ibn 'Arabi*, chapters 3-6.

24. Falconar, op. cit., p. 7.

25. Coleridge, *Miscellaneous Criticism*, ed. T.M. Raysor, p. 193.

26. Martin Buber, *I and Thou*, p. 103.

27. Blake, *The Laocoön Plate*.

28. Elémire Zolla, *Archetypes*, p. 33.

29. Corbin, *Creative Imagination in the Sufism of Ibn 'Arabi*, pp. 105-106.

30. Wordsworth, "I Wandered Lonely as a Cloud."

31. Steiner, *Knowledge of the Higher Worlds*, pp. 56, 64-66.

32. Corbin, *Creative Imagination*, pp. 105-106.

33. Frithjof Schuon, quoted in Nasr and Stoddart (eds.), *Religion of the Heart*, p. 288.

34. K. Okakura, *The Book of Tea*, p. 93.

35. Corbin, *Creative Imagination*, p. 107.

36. Blake, *Complete Works*, ed. G. Keynes, p. 633, 525.

37. Keats, *Endymion*, Book 1, lines 771-781.

38. Quoted in Corbin, *The Man of Light in Iranian Sufism*, p. 118.

39. Huston Smith, "Two Traditions—and Philosophy," in Nasr and Stoddart (eds.), *Religion of the Heart*, p. 289.

40. Corbin, *The Man of Light*, p. 116.

41. *The Divine Pymander of Hermes Trismegistus*, p. 12; Titus Burckhardt, *Alchemy*, pp. l96-201.

42. See Bachelard, *The Poetics of Reverie*, p. 114.

43. D.L. Snellgrove (ed.), *The Nine Ways of Bon*, pp. 19, 24.

44. See Ibn 'Arabi, "*Whoso Knoweth Himself...*," p. 21; *Kernel of the Kernel*, p. 10.

45. T. S. Eliot, *Four Quartets*.

46. Rene Guénon, *The Lord of the World*, p. 41.

47. Corbin, *Spiritual Body and Celestial Earth*, pp. 71-72.

48. Guénon, op. cit., pp. 27, 58; Corbin, *The Man of Light*, chapter IV.

49. Guénon, op. cit., p. 27n.

50. See Kathleen Raine, "The Vertical Dimension," *Temenos* 13, pp. 195-213.

51. Falconar, op. cit., pp. 139, 146.

52. William Blake, prelude to the *Book of Urizen*.

53. See Sangharakshita, *Alternative Traditions*, pp. 190-195; and Fremantle and Trungpa (tr. and ed.), *The Tibetan Book of the Dead*, pp. 103-105, 117, 151, 193.

54. Quoted in Falconar, op. cit., p. 179.

55. Cf. E.G. Howe, *The Mind of the Druid*, chapter 11.

56. See Jonathan Cott, *Stockhausen: Conversations with the Composer*, pp. 27, 125.

---

57. Quoted in Corbin, *The Man of Light,* p. 63.

58. Richard Holmes, op. cit., pp. 149-50.

59. Ibid., pp. 248-9, 292, 338, 651, 683-686.

60. E.G. Howe, op. cit., p. 6.

61. Corbin, *Avicenna,* pp. 178-183.

62. Blake, *The Marriage of Heaven and Hell; The Book of Thel; Visions of the Daughters of Albion.*

63. Llewellyn Vaughan-Lee, *The Call and the Echo,* p. 60.

CHAPTER 8

1. Ted Hughes, *Winter Pollen: Occasional Prose,* p. 441.

2. Henry Corbin, *The Man of Light in Iranian Sufism,* p. 115.

3. J. G. Bennett, *Deeper Man,* pp. 232ff.

4. Rumi, tr. by Coleman Barks, *Delicious Laughter,* p. 64.

5. See Jack Kornfield (ed.), *Teachings of the Buddha,* pp. 25, 45, 132, 181, 200.

6. David Bohm, *Unfolding Meaning,* p. 170.

7. See J. G. Bennett, *Deeper Man,* pp. 29, 33-34, 88, 112, 141, 143; *Sex,* pp. 36-40; also K. Okakura, *The Book of Tea,* p. 110.

8. See Ibn 'Arabi, *Fusus al Hikam,* tr. by Bulent Rauf, Introduction.

9. Ibid.

10. See T. Isutzu, *Sufism and Taoism: a Comparative Study.*

11. See Llewellyn Vaughan-Lee, *The Call and the Echo,* pp. 58-59.

12. See Corbin, *Creative Imagination,* pp. 112-135.

13. Philip Sherrard, in Nasr and Stoddart (eds.), *Religion of the Heart,* p. 265.

14. See William Chittick, "A Sufi approach to Religious Diversity," in Nasr and Stoddart, op. cit., pp. 50-90.

15. See, for example, Jack Kornfield (ed.), op. cit., pp. 23, 25, 53, 200, 203.

16. See David Bohm, *Unfolding Meaning,* p. 171.

17. Ibid., pp. 150-153; See also B. Rauf, *Addresses,* chapter 2.

18. David Bohm, op. cit., p. 171.

19. Philip Sherrard, in Nasr and Stoddart (eds), op. cit. p. 265.

20. Bohm, op. cit. p. 157.

21. Coleridge, "Dejection: an Ode," lines 50-58.

---

22. Jakob Böhme, ed. R. Waterfield, *Essential Readings,* p. 61.

23. Jonathan Cott, *Stockhausen: Conversations with the Composer,* pp. 74, 75.

24. In Nasr and Stoddart (eds.), op. cit., p. 274.

25. Ibid.

26. "Letter to Sara Hutchinson."

27. Ibn 'Arabi, tr. and ed. R.A. Nicholson, *Tarjuman al Ashwaq (The Interpreter of Ardent Desires).*

28. Keats, letter to Benjamin Bailey, 22 November 1817.

29. Vaughan-Lee, op. cit., p. 71.

30. Blake, "The Little Black Boy," *Songs of Innocence.*

31. Corbin, *Creative Imagination,* p. 301.

32. See Bohm, op. cit. p. 164.

33. Quoted in Vaughan-Lee, op. cit., p. 60.

34. Sri Krishna Menon, *Atma Darshan (At the Ultimate),* chapters 10, 11, 14, 17, 19.

35. Rumi, *Mathnawi* book 3, quoted in R. A. Nicholson (ed. and tr.), *Translations of Eastern Poetry and Prose,* p. 155.

36. See Eric Toms, *Holistic Logic,* chapters 5 and 6.

37. See David Bohm, op. cit., p. 152.

38. Vaughan-Lee, op. cit., p. 92.

39. See Owen Barfield, *The Light of the World.*

40. Coleridge, "Dejection: an Ode," line 47.

41. Jack Kornfield (ed.), op. cit., pp. 4-5.

42. Georg Kühlewind, *Working with Anthroposophy,* p. 22.

43. Vaughan-Lee, op. cit., p. 92.

44. See Herbert Guenther, *Meditation Differently,* chapter 3; Namkhai Norbu Rinpoche, *Rigbai Kujyug: The Six Vajra Verses,* chapters 2 and 3; Sogyal Rinpoche, *The Tibetan Book of Living and Dying,* chapter 10.

45. Wordsworth, "Lines Written a Few Miles above Tintern Abbey," line 96.

46. See K. Okakura, *The Book of Tea,* chapters 1 and 2.

47. Rumi, tr. Coleman Barks, op. cit., p. 138.

48. Vaughan-Lee, op. cit., p. 71.

EPILOGUE

1. See Robert Romanyshyn, *Technology as Symptom and Dream,* chapters 2, 3, 6, and 7; Titus Burckhardt, *Mirror of the Intellect,* chapter 2.

2. Thich Nhat Hanh, *The Song of No Coming No Going*, p. 18. See also David Bohm, *Unfolding Meaning*, chapters 1 and 5.

3. *Temenos*, A Review devoted to the Arts of the Imagination, 1980-1992, 13 vols. See, for example, Philip Sherrard, "Art and the Sacred," no. 2 (1982), p. 45; Joseph Pieper, "Work — Free Time — Leisure," no. 3 (1982), p. 149; Peter Malekin, "Art and the Liberation of the Mind," no. 5 (1984), p. 139; Pupul Jayakar, "Crisis in Culture," no. 6 (1985), p. 41; Pierre Emmanuel, "The Poetic Act and the Contemplative Regard," no. 7 (1986), p. 9; Henry Corbin, "The Theory of Visionary Knowledge in Islamic Philosophy," no. 8 (1987), p. 224; E.W.F. Tomlin, "Some Concepts of the Sacred and the Secular," no. 8, p. 204; Jean Louis Vieillard, "The Power of Images and the 'Productive Heart,'" no. 9 (1988), p. 168; Sisirkumar Ghose, "Poetry and Liberation: A point of View," no. 9, p. 189; Brian Keeble, "Work and the Sacred," no. 9, p. 235; Kathleen Raine, "Nature: House of the Soul," no. 9, p. 251; Keith Critchlow, "Cosmos as Order and Adornment," no. 10 (1989), p. 5; Peter Malekin, "Imagination: The Reality of the Future," no. 11 (1990), p. 194; Kathleen Raine, "Poetry as Prophecy," no. 11, p. 223; Sisirkumar Ghose, "Towards Ontic Poetry," no. 12 (1991), p. 54; Wilson Harris, "The Unfinished Genesis of the Imagination," no. 13 (1992), p. 69.

4. Eugene Jolas, Samuel Beckett et al, "Verticalist Manifesto," reprinted in Dougald McMillan, *Transition 1927-38: History of a Literary Era*, p. 66.

5. See René Guénon, *The Reign of Quantity and Signs of the Times*, 1972, chapters 1-18, 38-40.

6. Toshihiko Isutzu, *Creation and the timeless order of Things: Essays in Islamic Mystical Philosophy*, p. 2. See also Eric Toms, *Holistic Logic: a formalization of metaphysics*, chapters 1, 5, and 6.

7. On Deism, see Peter Byrne, *Natural Religion and the Nature of Religion*. Also Fritjof Capra, *The Tao of Physics*, chapters 3, 4, 10, 13, 18.

8. Edward Tenner, *New Technology and the Revenge Effect—Why Things Bite Back*.

9. Claudio Naranjo, *Character and Neurosis: An IntegrativeView*, 1995.

10. Isutzu (op. cit., chapters 1 and 3) provides a condensed account of the school of *wahdat al wujud* in Sufism. An account given by *advaita* is Ramana Maharshi, tr. S.S. Cohen, *Forty Verses on Reality*.

11. Arthur Koestler, *The Ghost in the Machine*; R. V. O'Neil, D. L. de Angelis, J. B. Wade, and T. F. H. Allen, *Hierarchichal Concept of Ecosystems*; T. F. H. Allen and T. B. Starr, *Hierarchy: Perspectives for Ecological Complexity*.

12. See S. T. Coleridge, *Biographia Literaria,* chapter XII, Thesis III-X.

13. Ludwig Wittgenstein, *Philosophical Investigations,* p. 213.

14. See Isutzu, op. cit., pp. 66-97.

15. Frithjof Schuon, *Sufism: Veil and Quintessence,* chapters 6 and 7.

16. P. B. Shelley, *Prometheus Unbound* (1819), Act II, scene iv. line 116.

17. See Titus Burckhardt, *Mirror of the Intellect,* chapters 2 and 12. See also Burckhardt, *Alchemy.*

18. Hellmut Wilhelm, *Change: Eight Lectures,* chapters 1-3.

19. Marcus B. Hester, *The Meaning of Poetic Metaphor,* Introduction.

BIBLIOGRAPHY

This list contains works cited and other relevant works. It is not exhaustive. Dates in square brackets indicate a more recent printing.

I. Anonymous and Traditional Works

Apocrypha, London, SPCK, 1935.

The Chaldean Oracles of Zoroaster, ed. W. Wynn Westcott, with an introduction by Kathleen Raine, Wellingborough, Aquarian, 1983.

The Fragments of Heraclitus, The Greek text with a new English translation, Bray, the Guild Press, 1976.

The Divine Pymander of Hermes Trismegistus, Godalming, The Fintry Trust, 1923 [1978].

Tao Te Ching [Lao Tse] with Wang Pi's *Commentary,* translated by Paul J. Lin, Ann Arbor, Michigan, 1977.

The Tibetan Book of the Dead, Trungpa and Fremantle (eds.), Boston, Shambhala, 1972 [1993].

The Upanishads, tr. J. Mascaro, Harmondsworth, Penguin, 1988.

The Upanishads, tr. W. B. Yeats and Shree Purohit Swami, London, Faber and Faber, 1937 [1975].

The Urga Manuscript. A Letter from Do Ring (Scribe to the Panchen Lama of Tibet) to Wing On, His Friend, Concerning the Inner Life. Gerrards Cross, Colin Smythe, 1976.

Zohar. The Book of Splendor, ed. and intr. Gershom Scholem, New York, Schocken, 1949 [1977].

II. Other Works

Affifi, A. (ed.), *Fusus al Hikam of Ibn 'Arabi,* with commentary, Beirut, 1946.

Aivanhov, O. M., *Aquarius: Herald of the Golden Age,* Fréjus, Editions Prosveta, 1981.

Allen, T. F. H., with T.B. Starr, *Hierarchy: Perspectives for Ecological Complexity,* Chicago, University of Chicago Press, 1988.

Arasteh, A. R., *Growth to Selfhood,* London, Routledge and Kegan Paul, 1980.

Bachelard, G., *A Psychoanalysis of Fire*, Boston, Beacon, 1964 [1968].

———— tr. C. Gaudin, *On Poetic Imagination and Reverie*, Dallas, Spring Publications, 1987.

———— *The Poetics of Reverie*, Boston, Beacon, 1971.

———— tr. M. Jolas, *The Poetics of Space*, Boston, Beacon, 1971.

Barfield, O., *History in English Words*, London, Methuen, 1926.

———— *The Light of the World* (Supplement to *Anthroposophical Movement* February 1954), London, Rudolf Steiner Press, 1954.

———— *Owen Barfield and the Origin of Language*, New York, St. George Publications, 1978.

———— *Poetic Diction*, London, Faber and Gwyer, 1928.

———— *The Rediscovery of Meaning and Other Essays*, Middletown, Conn., Wesleyan University Press, 1989.

———— *Romanticism Comes of Age*, London, Rudolf Steiner Press, 1966. [1990]

———— *Saving the Appearances: A Study in Idolatry*, London, Faber and Faber, 1957 [Wesleyan University Press, 1988].

———— *What Coleridge Thought*, London, Oxford University Press, 1971.

Bennett, J. G., ed. A.G.E. Blake, *Deeper Man*, London, Turnstone Books, 1978 [1985, 1995].

———— *Needs of a New Age Community*, Sherborne, Coombe Springs Press, 1977.

———— *Studies From the Dramatic Universe*, 3 vols, Sherborne, Springs Press, 1976-78.

———— *A Spiritual Psychology*, Lakemont, Georgia, CSA Press, 1974.

———— *Transformation*, Sherborne, Coombe Springs Press, 1978.

———— *Sex: The Relationship between Sex and Spiritual Development*, York Beach, Weiser, 1981.

Benz, E., tr. B. R. Reynolds and E. M. Paul, *The Mystical Sources of German Romantic Philosophy*, Allison Park, Penn., Pickwick Publications, 1968 [1983].

Blair, L., *Rhythms of Vision: The Changing Patterns of Belief*, London, Croom Helm, 1975.

Blake, A. G. E., *A Seminar on Time*, Charles Town, West Virginia, Claymont Communications, 1980.

Blake, W., ed. Max Plowman, *Poems and Prophecies*, London, Dent/Everyman, 1926 [intr. Kathleen Raine, 1975].

———— ed. Geoffrey Keynes, *Complete Writings*, Oxford, Oxford University Press, 1966.

———— ed. D. V. Erdman and H. Bloom, *The Poetry and Prose of William Blake*, New York, Doubleday and Co., 1970.

————

Bohm, D., *Unfolding Meaning: a Weekend of Dialogue with David Bohm,* London and New York, Routledge/Ark, 1985 [1987].

———— *Wholeness and the Implicate Order,* London and New York, Routledge, 1980 [Ark, 1981].

Böhme, J., ed. Robin Waterfield, *Essential Readings,* Wellingborough, Crucible, 1989.

Bortoft, H., *Goethe's Scientific Consciousness,* Tunbridge Wells, Institute for Cultural Research, 1986.

Bragdon, C., *The Eternal Poles,* London, Rider & Co., n.d.

Bryce, D., *The Symbolism of the Celtic Cross,* Llanerch, 1989.

Buber, M., tr. R. G. Smith, *I and Thou,* Edinburgh, T. and T. Clark, 1953.

Burckhardt, T., tr. W. Stoddart, *Alchemy: Science of the Cosmos, Science of the Soul,* London, Watkins, 1967 [Shaftesbury, Element, 1986].

———— tr. and ed. W. Stoddart, *Mirror of the Intellect: Essays on Traditional Science and Sacred Art,* New York, SUNY Press, 1987.

Campbell, J. (ed.), *Myths, Dreams and Religion,* Dallas, Spring Publications, 1970 [1989].

Capra, F., *The Tao of Physics,* London, Fontana/Collins, 1975.

Chittick, W. C., *The Sufi Path of Knowledge,* New York, SUNYPress, 1989.

Coleridge, S. T., *Miscellanies: Theory of Life,* London, Bell, 1911.

———— *Biographia Literaria: Lay Sermons,* London, Bell, 1895.

———— *The Friend,* London, Bell, 1896.

———— *Poetry and Prose,* ed. and intr. K. Raine, London, Penguin, 1957 [1990].

———— *Selected Poems,* ed. and intr. John Beer, London, Dent/Everyman, 1992.

———— *Table Talk,* London and New York, Routledge, 1884.

Collin, R., *Theory of Celestial Influence,* London, Vincent Stuart, 1954 [Routledge Ark, 1995].

Corbin, H., tr. W. R. Trask, *Avicenna and the Visionary Recital,* Princeton, Princeton University Press, 1960 [1990].

———— tr. R. Manheim, *Creative Imagination in the Sufism of Ibn 'Arabi,* Princeton, Princeton University Press, 1969 [1981].

———— tr. R. Manheim and J. Morris, *Cyclical Time and Ismaili Gnosis,* London, Kegan Paul International, 1983.

———— tr. N. Pearson, *The Man of Light in Iranian Sufism,* New York, Omega Publications, 1994.

———— tr. N. Pearson, *Spiritual Body and Celestial Earth,* Princeton, Princeton University Press, 1977.

——— tr. P. and L. Sherrard, *Temple and Contemplation*, London, Kegan Paul International, 1986.

Cott, J., (ed.), *Stockhausen: Conversations with the Composer*, London, Picador, 1974.

Couliano, I., tr. H. S. Wiesner and Ioan P. Couliano, *The Tree of Gnosis: Gnostic Mythology from early Christianity to Modern Nihilism*, HarperSanFrancisco, 1990.

Cranston, S. L., with J. Head (eds.), *Reincarnation in World Thought*, New York, Julian Press, 1967.

Einstein, A., *Ideas and Opinions*, New York, Dell Publishers, 1973.

Eliot, T. S., *Four Quartets*, London, Faber and Faber, 1944 [1979].

Falconar, A. E. I., *Sufi Literature and the Journey to Immortality*, Delhi, Motilal Banarsidass, and Isle of Man, Non-Aristotelian Publishing, 1991.

Al-Ghazzali, tr. and intr. W. H. T. Gairdner, *The Mishkat al Anwar [Niche for Lights] of Al-Ghazzali* (1923), [New Delhi, Kitab Bhavan, 1991].

——— tr. A. Hazarvi, *The Mystery of the Human Soul*, Lahore, Sh. Muhammad Ashraf, 1981.

Goethe, J. W. von, *Farbenlehre*, in *Schriften über die Natur, Werke*, Band 62, Stuttgart, Kröner, 1949.

——— *Maximen und Reflexionen*, *Gesamtausgabe*, Band 21, Munich, DTV, 1963.

——— *Der West-östliche Diwan*, *Gesamtausgabe*, Band 5, Munich, DTV, 1963.

Guénon, R., tr. P. Kingsley, *The Great Triad*, Cambridge, Quinta Essentia, 1991.

——— tr. A. Cheke, A. Blake, C. Shaffer and O. de Nottbeck, *The Lord of the World*, Ellingstring, Coombe Springs Press, 1983.

——— tr. Lord Northbourne, *The Reign of Quantity and the Signs of the Times*, London, Luzac, 1953 [Baltimore, N.J., Penguin Books, 1972].

Guenther, H., *Meditation Differently: Phenomenological-psychological Aspects of Tibetan Buddhist (Mahamudra and sNying-thig) Practices from Original Tibetan Sources*, Delhi, Motilal Banarsidass, 1992.

Guirdham, A., *Man: Divine or Social*, London, Vincent Stuart, 1960.

Gurdjieff, G. I., *Life is real only then, when "I am"* (All *and Everything Third Series*), New York, Viking Penguin, 1991.

Hanh, Thich Nhat, *The Song of No Coming No Going*, Leeds, Being Books, 1996.

Harvey, A., *The Way of Passion: a Celebration of Rumi*, Berkeley, Cal., Frog Ltd., 1994.

———

Hester, M. B., *The Meaning of Poetic Metaphor,* The Hague and Paris, 1967.

Hodgson, A. M., *Crisis in the Search for Truth,* High Burton, Coombe Springs Press, 1984.

—— *Greater Sufism,* Ellingstring, Coombe Springs Press, 1982.

Hoeller, S., *The Gnostic Jung and the Seven Sermons to the Dead,* Wheaton, Ill., Madras and London, Quest Books, 1982 [1989].

Holmes, R., *Coleridge,* Oxford and New York, Oxford University Press, 1982 [1991].

—— *Shelley: The Pursuit,* London and Harmondsworth, Penguin Books, 1987.

—— (ed.), *Shelley on Love,* London, Anvil Press, 1980.

Howe, E. G., The Mind of the Druid, London, Skoob, 1989.

Hughes, T., ed. W. Scammell, *Winter Pollen: Occasional Prose,* London, Faber and Faber, 1994.

Huxley, A., *Island,* London, Grafton, 1976 [1985].

Iamblichus, ed. S. Neuville and tr. T. M. Johnson, *The Exhortation to Philosophy, including the Letters of Iamblichus and Proclus' Commentary on the Chaldean Oracles,* Grand Rapids, Michigan, Phanes Press, 1988.

Ibn 'Arabi, Muhyiddin, tr. Ralph Austin, *Bezels of Wisdom [Fusus al Hikam],* London and New York, SPCK, 1980.

—— ed. and tr. Titus Burckhardt and Angela Culme-Seymour, *Wisdom of the Prophets: Chapters from the Fusus al Hikam,* Sherborne, Beshara Publications, 1975.

—— tr. and with commentary by Ismail Hakki Bursevi and rendered into English by Bulent Rauf, with the help of R. Brass and H. Tollemache, *Fusus al Hikam,* 4 vols, Oxford, Istanbul and San Francisco, Muhyiddin Ibn 'Arabi Society, 1986-91.

—— *Kernel of the Kernel,* translation and commentary by Ismail Hakki Bursevi, Sherborne, Beshara Publications, n.d.

—— tr. and ed. R. A. Nicholson, *Tarjuman al Ashwaq [Interpreter of Ardent Desires]: A Collection of Mystical Odes,* London, Theosophical Publishing House, 1911 [1978].

—— tr. T. H. Weir, *"Whoso Knoweth Himself..." from the Treatise on Being [risalat al wujudivyah],* Sherborne and Abingdon, Beshara Publications, 1976 [1988].

Iraqi, Fakhruddin, tr. and ed. William Chittick and Peter Lamborn Wilson, *Divine Flashes [Lama 'at],* London and New Jersey, SPCK, 1982.

Isutzu, T., *Creation and the Timeless Order of Things,* Ashland, Oregon, White Cloud Press, 1994.

Jîlî, Abd' Al Karim Al, ed. and tr. Titus Burckhardt, *Universal Man*, Sherborne, Beshara Publications, 1983.

Kabitoglou, E. D., *Plato and the English Romantics: dialogoi*, London, Routledge, l990.

Keats, J., ed. R. Gittings, *Letters of John Keats: A Selection*, Oxford and London, Oxford University Press, 1970.

—— ed. J. Barnard, *The Complete Poems*, London, Penguin, 1979.

Knight, G., *The Rose Cross and the Goddess: A Quest for the Eternal Feminine Principle*, Wellingborough, Aquarian, 1985.

Koestler, A., *The Roots of Coincidence*, London, Picador, 1974.

Kornfield, J. (ed.), *Teachings of the Buddha*, New York and Boston, Shambhala, 1993.

Kühlewind, tr. and ed. G., M. Lipson and C. Bamford, *Working with Anthroposophy*, New York, Anthroposophic Press, 1992.

Kunisch, H. (ed.), *Eckhart, Tauler, Seuse: Ein Textbuch aus der Altdeutschen Mystik*, Hamburg, Rowohlt, 1958.

Lawrence, D. H., *Psychoanalysis and the Unconscious*, London, Secker and Warburg, 1923.

Lings, M., *Symbol and Archetype: a Study of the Meaning of Existence*, Cambridge, Quinta Essentia, 1991.

Lopez, D. S. (Jr.), *The Heart Sutra Explained: Indian and Tibetan Commentaries*, New York, SUNY Press, 1988.

Maharshi, R., tr. and with commentary by S. S. Cohen, *Forty Verses on Reality [Ulladu narpadu]*, London, Watkins, 1978.

—— *The Spiritual Teaching of Ramana Maharshi*, Boston, Shambhala, 1988.

Matchett, E., *Creative Action: The Making of Meaning in a Complex World*, London, Turnstone Books, 1975.

—— *Journeys of Nothing in the Land of Everything*, London, Turnstone Books, 1975.

McMillan, D., *Transition 1927-38: History of a Literary Era*, London, Calder and Boyars, 1975.

Menon, Sri Krishna, *Atma Darshan*, Austin, Texas, Advaita Publishers, 1989.

—— *Atma Nirvriti*, Austin, Texas, Advaita Publishers, 1990.

Merton, T., *Zen and the Birds of Appetite*, Boston, Shambhala, 1993.

Naranjo, C., *Character and Neurosis: an Integrative View*, Nevada, IDHHB/Gateways, 1994.

Nasr, S. H., *Man and Nature: The Spiritual Crisis in Modern Man*, London, Allen and Unwin, 1968 [1990].

Nasr, S. H. and W. Stoddart (eds.), *Religion of the Heart*, Washington, Foundation for Traditional Studies, 1991.

Nicholson, R. (ed. and tr.), intr. C. E. Bosworth, *Translations of Eastern Poetry and Prose*, New Jersey, Humanities Press, and London, Curzon Press, 1987.

Norbu Rinpoche, N., *The Crystal and the Way of Light: Sutra, Tantra, and Dzogchen*, London, Routledge, 1986.

―――― *Dzogchen*, London, Penguin Arkana, 1989.

―――― ed. C. Goh, *Rigbai Kujyug* [The Six Vajra Verses], Singapore, Rinchen, 1990.

Novalis (Friedrich van Hardenberg) tr. and ed. Arthur Versluis, *Pollen and Fragments: Selected Poetry and Prose*, Grand Rapids, Michigan, Phanes Press, 1989.

O'Neil, R.V., with D. L. de Angelis, J. B. Wade and T. F. H. Allen, *A Hierarchical Concept of Ecosystems*, New Jersey, Princeton University Press, 1986.

Okakura, K., *The Book of Tea*, London and Boston, Shambhala, 1993.

Ouspensky, P. D., *The Psychology of Man's Possible Evolution*, London, Routledge and Penguin Arkana, 1991.

Paracelsus, ed. Nicholas Goodrick-Clarke, *Essential Readings*, Wellingborough, Crucible, 1990.

Pirsig, R. M., *Lila: an Enquiry into Morals*, London and New York, Corgi, 1991.

Portuguès, P., *The Visionary Poetics of Allen Ginsberg*, Santa Barbara, Ross-Erikson, 1978.

Raine, K., *Blake and Antiquity*, London and Henley, Routledge and Kegan Paul, 1979.

―――― *Coleridge*, London, Longmans, Green and Co., 1953.

―――― *Defending Ancient Springs,* Ipswich, Golgonooza Press, 1985; and Hudson, N.Y., Lindisfarne Press, 1967.

―――― *Golgonooza, City of Imagination: Last Studies in William Blake*, Ipswich, Golgonooza Press, 1991; and Hudson, N.Y., Lindisfarne Press, 1991.

―――― *India Seen Afar*, Barnstaple, Green Books, 1990.

Raschke, H., *Der Innere Logos im Antiken und Deutschen Idealismus,* Bremen, Friedrich Trüjen Verlag, 1949.

Rauf, B., *Addresses*, Beshara Publications, 1986.

Reyner, J. H., *A Philosophy of Delight*, London, Watkins, 1976.

Romanyshyn, R., *Technology as Symptom and Dream*, London and New York, Routledge, 1989,

―――